saturday COOKS cookbook

Easy recipes from Britain's favourite chefs

saturday COOKS cookbook

Easy recipes from Britain's favourite chefs

Presented by **Antony Worrall Thompson**

itv 1 | saturday COOKS!

PROSPECT

MITCHELL BEAZLEY

Saturday Cooks Cookbook

Saturday Cooks is produced by Prospect Pictures, part of DCD Media plc.

First published in Great Britain in 2008 by
Mitchell Beazley,
An imprint of Octopus Publishing Group Limited,
2–4 Heron Quays, London E14 4JP.
An Hachette Livre UK Company
www.octopusbooks.co.uk

A CIP catalogue record for this book is available from the British Library.

ISBN: 978 1 84533 342 3

While all reasonable care has been taken during the preparation of this edition, neither the publisher, editors, contributors or authors can accept responsibility for any consequences arising from the use thereof or from the information contained therein.

Commissioning Editor: Rebecca Spry
Art Director: Tim Foster
Executive Art Editor: Yasia Williams-Leedham
Designer: Nicky Collings
Project Editor: Georgina Atsiaris
Editor: Orla Broderick
Prop Stylist: Joanne Harris
Home Economist: Clare Greenstreet
Photographer: Steve Lee
Production Manager: Peter Hunt
Proofreader: Debbie Robertson
Indexer: Diana LeCore

Typeset in The Sans

Printed and bound by Toppan in China

With thanks to the whole team at Prospect Pictures and Saturday Cooks.

Acknowledgements
Grateful acknowledgement is made for permission to reprint recipes from the following previously published works: Oriental Pork Chops, Char Sui Pork from *China Modern* by Ching-He Huang, with permission from Kyle Cathie Ltd; Halibut Curry from *Easy Indian Cookbook* by Manju Malhi, with permission from Duncan Baird; Linguine with Prawns, Melanzane alla Parmigiana, Deep Fried Polenta, Panforte, Limoncello Tart from *Fantastico* by Gino D'Acampo, with permission from Kyle Cathie Ltd; Chilli Crusted Steak, Slow Roast Pork, Thai-style Chicken Prawn and Corn Cakes from *The Feel Good Cook Book* by Ainsley Harriott, with permission from Random House publishers; Prawn and Coconut Satay Broth, Lamb Cutlets with Pea and Chickpea Mash from *In the Mood for Food* by Jo Pratt, with permission from Penguin Books Ltd; Seabass and Leek Carbonara from *Keeping it Simple* by Gary Rhodes, with permission from Penguin Books Ltd; Lamb Bobotie from *Leith's Cookery Course* by Prue Leith, © Leith's Farm; Black Pepper Chicken Curry from *Simply Indian* by Atul Kochhar, with permission from Quadrille; Southern Fried Chicken from *Soul in a Bowl* by Momma Cherri, with permission from Absolute Press; Rack of Lamb with Pistachio Crust, Thai Beef Salad from *The Top 100 recipes from Food and Drink* by Antony Worrall Thompson, with permission from BBC Books; Lamb Fillet with Flageolet Beans from *Wild Flavours* by Mike Robinson, with permission from Cassell Illustrated.

The author and publisher apologize for any errors or omissions in the above list and would be grateful to be notified of any corrections that should be incorporated in a reprint.

Find out more about all the *Saturday Cooks* chefs at www.cooksforcooks.com

contents

Foreword by Antony Worrall Thompson

It's 4.30am on Saturday and the noise would wake the dead as three alarm clocks go off in unattractive harmony...it's that time again when I can't afford to be late, it's *Saturday Cooks* time. A blast of hot water followed by 2 minutes of ice-cold from the power shower shakes me into reality. I shoot into my rehearsal clothes, grab a banana and a cup of mint tea and I'm ready to attack the M4 on my drive to Wandsworth.

I arrive at Capital Studios just after 6am. The drive has been a dream, almost zero traffic – a luxury on the M4 – and just me and the radio. It's a quick studio breakfast, then a script read-through with a full cook-on rehearsal starting at 7.45am. Every dish is rehearsed in full, to perfect timings. Set, lights, build up the adrenalin, check camera positions – and of course make-up!

I have lovely guests on each show, mostly chefs who understand the *Saturday Cooks* philosophy – keep it simple, keep it seasonal and make it delicious. And

then, of course, there's my *Saturday Cooks* friend, the Meals on Reels slot machine, where each guest gets three random ingredients with which to produce a dish in six minutes at the end of the show. Some chefs love the challenge, some just pray that the public won't vote for them! This is the only part of the show where the cooking is not rehearsed, as the chefs would never get the same ingredients twice.

Assuming that rehearsals go according to plan, we get about 20 minutes to relax, check our notes, and patch up the make-up and then we're ready to go. A quick rehearsal for the opening of our show, a couple of deep breaths and then those wonderful words coming through my earpiece 'have a great show, we're live on air, 21 seconds on titles...' There's no going back, this is live TV.

Enjoy these excellent dishes and remember Saturday is chill-out day – pop down to the shops and get stuck into your favourite foods.

beef

CHILLI CRUSTED STEAK WITH CRUSHED POTATOES

This is a simple dish but a real masterpiece. The crushed potatoes are a kind of textured mash that you often see in trendy restaurants; don't be tempted to make them too smooth. Pile them into a metal cooking ring set on the serving plate for a really professional result.

600g (1lb 5oz) new potatoes
3 tbsp olive oil
4 fillet steaks, each about
    115g (4oz)
salt and freshly ground black pepper

FOR THE CHILLI CRUST
175g (6oz) fresh white breadcrumbs
2 garlic cloves, peeled
2 birds eye chillies, stems removed
2 fresh thyme sprigs
about 3 tbsp Dijon mustard
55g (2oz) butter

FOR THE HERB OIL
small bunch fresh chives
handful fresh parsley leaves
1 fresh thyme sprig, leaves stripped off
about 6 tbsp extra virgin olive oil

. . . .

Serves 4

Cook the new potatoes in a pan of boiling salted water for 15–20 minutes or until tender.

To make the herb oil, put the chives into a mini-blender with the parsley and thyme. Add the olive oil and season to taste. Blitz until you have a bright green oil, adding a little more oil if necessary for a pouring consistency.

Meanwhile, heat a large heavy-based frying pan. Rub a little olive oil into the steaks and season to taste. Add to the hot frying pan and cook for a minute or two on each side until nicely browned. If you prefer your meat more well done then cook for a few minutes longer on each side.

To make the chilli crust, place the breadcrumbs, garlic, chilli and thyme into a food processor or liquidizer and blitz together. Add the remaining olive oil and season to taste, then blitz again until evenly blended. Tip onto a flat plate.

Brush about a teaspoon of the mustard on one side of each of the steaks. Then place the steaks, one at a time, mustard side down onto to the chilli crumbs and cover thickly.

Add a couple of knobs of butter to the frying pan and return the steaks to the pan, crust side down. Cook for about 2 minutes or until the crust is crisp and golden brown. Transfer to a warmed plate and leave to rest for at least 1 minute.

Drain the potatoes and add the remaining butter and mustard, then season to taste. Crush gently with a fork or potato crusher, ensuring that you still have a bit of texture left in the potatoes.

Arrange the crushed new potatoes on warmed plates and put a chilli crusted steak on top of each one. Drizzle around the herb oil and serve at once.

MINUTE PROVENCAL BEEF

When I think of Provence I recall long leisurely meals under the shade of a tree, eating simple food made from the highest quality ingredients. I'd serve this beef with a fresh, crisp green salad and a glass of light fruity wine – perfect for a summer's evening when time is not on your side.

4 red peppers
3 tbsp olive oil
2 x 400g cans chopped tomatoes
1 tsp light muscovado sugar
2 onions, finely sliced
4 sirloin steaks, trimmed and
  cut into strips
1 tbsp sherry vinegar
handful fresh mixed herbs (such as
  chives, parsley and basil), roughly
  chopped
salt and freshly ground black pepper

. . . .

Serves 4

Preheat the oven to 180C/350F/Gas 4. Cut the peppers in half and remove the cores, then place four of the halves in a small roasting tin and drizzle over a tablespoon of the olive oil. Roast for 15–20 minutes until just tender but still holding their shape. Finely slice the remaining peppers and set aside.

Pour the tomatoes into a pan with the sugar. Cook for about 10 minutes until well reduced and thickened, stirring occasionally.

Heat two large frying pans. Add a tablespoon of the olive oil to one of the heated pans and then tip in the onions. Sauté for a couple of minutes until softened. Add the reserved sliced red peppers and continue to sauté for another 5 minutes or so until the peppers are cooked through and tender.

Add the remaining tablespoon of olive oil to the second frying pan and then add the beef. Cook for a few minutes until sealed and lightly browned. When the beef is cooked to your liking, sprinkle over the sherry vinegar, tossing to coat evenly.

Tip the onion and pepper mixture into the beef with the reduced tomatoes and mix thoroughly. Season to taste.

Spoon the Provençal beef into the roasted pepper halves and arrange on warmed plates. Scatter over the herbs and serve at once.

ROAST BEEF FILLET WITH PLUM SAUCE AND SOY ROAST POTATOES

The beef can be marinated for up to 24 hours in the fridge, but it's important to allow the joint to come back up to room temperature before you cook it. For the best flavour choose a fillet that is marbled with fat and has been hung for at least three weeks. Ask your butcher for the chateaubriand, which is taken from the thick end of the fillet.

Mix together the light soy sauce, kecap manis, rice wine, garlic and a pinch of Sichuan pepper in a non-metallic dish that fits the beef snugly. Add the beef and turn to coat. Cover with cling film and leave to marinate for at least an hour at room temperature.

Preheat the oven to 240C/475F/Gas 9. Cut the new potatoes in half and cook in a pan of boiling salted water for 10–15 minutes or until tender. Drain and tip into a roasting tin. Drizzle over half of the olive oil and season with salt and Sichuan pepper. Roast for 10–15 minutes until crispy, tossing twice to ensure even cooking. Drizzle over the dark soy sauce and return to the oven for 5 minutes until caramelized. Add a squeeze of lime.

Meanwhile, drain the beef, reserving the marinade. Heat a heavy-based frying pan, add the remaining olive oil and seal the beef on all sides until brown – about 6 minutes over a high heat. Transfer to a roasting tin lined with foil coming up over the sides and drizzle over the marinade. Close up the foil to form a loose parcel around the beef and roast for 8 minutes, then open up the foil and roast for another 3 minutes for medium-rare, or longer to your liking. Remove from the oven and leave to rest in a warm place for 10 minutes.

Transfer the juices from the beef back to the frying pan and bring to a gentle simmer. Add the plums and cook for about 5 minutes until completely softened, stirring occasionally.

Heat the vegetable oil in a wok. Add the French beans and deep-fry for 2–3 minutes until tender but not coloured. Remove with a slotted spoon and drain on kitchen paper. Carefully drain off the oil from the wok leaving a small amount behind. Add the garlic and chilli and stir-fry for 1 minute. Tip the beans back in, tossing well. Season with salt and drizzle over the hoisin sauce.

Carve the beef into slices and arrange on warmed plates. Drizzle over the plum sauce and serve with the potatoes and beans.

2 tbsp light soy sauce

75ml (2 ½ fl oz) kecap manis (sweet soy sauce)

75ml (2 ½ fl oz) rice wine

6 garlic cloves, thinly sliced

about 1 ¼ tsp freshly ground Sichuan pepper

750g (1lb 10oz) beef fillet, in one piece

1kg (2lb 4oz) new potatoes

good pinch salt

150ml (¼ pint) olive oil

5 tbsp dark soy sauce

squeeze of lime juice

6 ripe plums, stoned and halved

500ml (18fl oz) vegetable oil

250g (9oz) French beans, trimmed

2 garlic cloves, halved

1 red chilli, halved, seeded and finely chopped

2 tbsp hoisin sauce

Serves 4

STEAK AU POIVRE AND CHIPS

This French classic has stood the test of time. For me, the occasional piece of red meat served with a rich, creamy sauce and some fat chunky chips is delicious. Remember the motto: 'Everything in moderation, and a little in excess.' A refreshing watercress salad on the side is the perfect accompaniment.

4 x 150g (5oz) filet mignon (centre-cut fillet steaks)
2 tbsp coarsely ground black pepper
1 tbsp olive oil
25g (1oz) butter
4 tbsp brandy
4 tbsp white wine
125ml (4fl oz) beef stock
2 tbsp green peppercorns (in brine)
125ml (4fl oz) double cream

FOR THE CHIPS
4 large baking potatoes, scrubbed and cut into chunky chips
4 tbsp olive oil
6 garlic cloves, skin on but slightly crushed
salt and freshly ground black pepper

. . . .

Serves 4

Preheat the oven to 220C/425F/Gas 7. To make the chips, place the potatoes in a large freezer bag with the olive oil and garlic. Season to taste, then seal the bag and shake until all of the potatoes are evenly coated. Tip onto a large non-stick baking sheet and roast for 25–30 minutes until the potatoes are cooked through and crisp, turning occasionally to ensure that they cook evenly.

When ready to cook the steaks, heat a large heavy-based frying pan. Season the steaks generously with the coarsely ground black pepper. Add the oil and a knob of the butter to the pan and as soon as the butter stops foaming, add the steaks. Cook for 2–4 minutes on each side, depending on how rare you like your steak. Transfer the steaks to a warm plate, season with salt and set aside in a warm place to rest for 5 minutes.

Pour away the excess fat from the pan. Pour in the brandy and flambé to burn off the alcohol, scraping the meat juices from the bottom of the pan. Pour in the white wine and allow to reduce by half. Add the stock and continue to cook until the sauce is well reduced, stirring occasionally. Stir in the green peppercorns, cream and remaining butter and cook for a further 2 minutes until you have a nice sauce consistency.

Pile the chips on a plate and top each with a steak. Pour over the pepper sauce and serve at once.

MARINATED BEEF FILLET WITH MUSTARD AND PARSLEY

This is a nice twist on the traditional way of cooking this cut, which is taken from the thick end of the fillet. Marinating meat is one of the best ways to give it more flavour and to tenderize it at the same time.

700g (1lb 9oz) beef fillet, from centre in one piece
1 tbsp olive oil
55g (2oz) butter, diced
2 shallots, finely chopped
1 tsp corn flour
50ml (2fl oz) dry sherry
300ml (½ pint) beef stock
2 tbsp wholegrain mustard
2 tbsp chopped fresh flat-leaf parsley
buttered cabbage, to serve

FOR THE MARINADE
2 garlic cloves
2 fresh thyme sprigs
1 fresh rosemary sprig
3 tbsp sherry vinegar
1 tsp crushed peppercorns
5 tbsp olive oil

. . . .

Serves 4

Roughly chop the garlic, thyme and rosemary. Tip it into a shallow non-metallic dish that fits the beef joint snugly and stir in the vinegar, peppercorns and olive oil.

Tie the beef fillet at 2.5cm (1 inch) intervals with butchers string and put it into the marinade, turning to coat. Cover with cling film and chill for 12 hours, turning occasionally to ensure that the flavours penetrate evenly.

Preheat the oven to 200C/400F/Gas 6. Remove the meat from the marinade and wipe dry. Allow to return to room temperature. Reserve the remaining marinade to use in the sauce.

Heat an ovenproof frying pan and add the olive oil, then seal the beef fillet all over. Transfer to the oven and roast for 15 minutes for rare, longer if you prefer your meat well done. Remove from the oven and transfer to a warm plate. Set aside to rest for 10 minutes or so.

Meanwhile, melt half of the butter in a small pan and sweat the shallots for a few minutes until softened but not coloured.

Drain off the excess fat from the roasting tin. Add the corn flour, the remaining marinade and the sherry, whisking until smooth. Place the tin directly on the hob and bring to a simmer, scraping the bottom of the pan to remove any sediment. Strain into the shallots and then reduce by two-thirds, stirring occasionally.

Pour the stock into the reduced liquid and bring to the boil. Remove from the heat and whisk in the remaining butter, the mustard and parsley. Season to taste.

Carve the rested beef fillet into eight medallions. Place the buttered cabbage on warm plates and put two slices of beef on each one. Let everyone help themselves to the sauce.

BRAISED BEEF ROLLS WITH CRUSHED NEW POTATO AND PARMESAN GRATIN

The slow cooking of the stuffed beef rolls results in an intensely flavoured, meltingly tender dish. The lining of the cooked ham inside the beef is especially important to the flavour.

Preheat the oven to 170C/325F/Gas 3. Soak the bread in water for 1 minute, then squeeze dry and chop finely. Tip into a bowl and add the onion, carrot, celery, parsley, Parmesan, egg and thyme. Season to taste and mix well to combine.

Cover the steak slices with cling film and flatten out with a steak hammer or rolling pin to a 3mm (⅛ inch) thickness. Place a piece of ham on each slice of beef, trimming them down as necessary and then spread the stuffing on top. Roll each one up into a sausage shape and secure with toothpicks.

Heat a heavy-based casserole dish that has a lid. Add the oil and quickly seal the beef rolls on all sides until lightly golden – you may have to do this in batches depending on the size of your dish.

Arrange the beef rolls in the casserole dish and pour in the wine. Add 50ml (2fl oz) of water, then cover and cook in the oven for 1½ hours or until the beef rolls are completely tender, adding a little more water if it looks like the beef is going to cook dry.

Meanwhile, preheat a separate oven to 200C/400F/Gas 6 to make the gratin. Cook the potatoes in a pan of boiling salted water for 15–20 minutes until tender. Drain well and return to the pan, then roughly crush with a fork and season to taste. Tip into a baking dish. Mix together the Parmesan and parsley and sprinkle over the potatoes, then drizzle the olive oil on top. Roast for 8–10 minutes or until bubbling and lightly golden.

Arrange the stuffed beef rolls on warmed plates and spoon over a little of the remaining juices. Place the crushed new potato and Parmesan gratin on the table and let everyone help themselves.

1 thick slice white bread
1 small onion, finely chopped
1 small carrot, finely chopped
½ celery stick, finely chopped
1 tbsp chopped fresh flat-leaf parsley
55g (2oz) freshly grated Parmesan
1 egg, beaten
½ tsp fresh thyme leaves
4 x 115g (4oz) thick slices rump or topside beef
4 slices cooked ham
2 tbsp olive oil
50ml (2fl oz) white wine
salt and freshly ground black pepper

FOR THE GRATIN
450g (1lb) new potatoes, halved
50g (1¾oz) freshly grated Parmesan
6 tbsp chopped fresh flat-leaf parsley
2 tbsp olive oil

Serves 4

STEAK AND KIDNEY PUDDING

I just love this traditional pudding even if it does require a little attention. I like to make it from scratch so that the delicious meat juices soak into the suet pastry as the whole thing cooks. Serve it with creamy mashed potatoes and buttered peas.

Butter a 1.2 litre (2 pint) pudding basin or Pyrex bowl and line the base with a disc of non-stick parchment paper. To make the suet pastry, place the suet in a bowl and sieve over the flour and turmeric, then mix gently. Season lightly and add the water, a little at a time, cutting through the mixture with a round-bladed knife. Use your hands to form a soft dough.

Roll out two-thirds of the pastry on a lightly floured work surface to a 5mm (¼ inch) thickness and use to line the prepared pudding basin, leaving at least 1cm (½ inch) of the pastry hanging over the edge. Roll out the remaining piece of pastry to a disc 2.5cm (1 inch) larger than the top and set aside.

Place the steak in a bowl with the kidneys. Season to taste and stir in the flour until evenly coated, then mix in the onion, garlic and parsley. Spoon into the lined pudding basin, being careful not to press it down, then pour over the claret and sprinkle the Worcestershire sauce on top. Insert a bay leaf into the middle of the pudding, then carefully pour in enough water to reach about two-thirds of the way to the top, but not covering the meat mixture completely.

Dampen the edges of the pastry lining the basin, place the lid over the filling and press down both edges together to seal. Trim off any excess pastry and make two small slits in the top. Cover the pudding with a disc of non-stick parchment paper and a double piece of foil, pleated in the centre to allow room for expansion while cooking. Secure it with string, making a handle so that you can lift the bowl out of the steamer easily.

Place the pudding on an upturned (upside-down) plate in a large pan filled two-thirds up the side of the basin with water. Cover and steam for 4–5 hours, adding boiling water occasionally to stop the pan boiling dry. Allow the cooked pudding to stand for 10 minutes, then cut the string and remove the foil and paper. Cover with a flat plate and carefully invert. Gently remove the basin and peel off the paper disc. Serve immediately.

butter, for greasing

450g (1lb) chuck beef steak, trimmed and cut into 1cm (½ inch) cubes

225g (8oz) ox or lamb's kidney, well trimmed and cut into 1cm (½ inch) cubes

2 tbsp plain flour

1 onion, diced

1 garlic clove, crushed

1 tbsp chopped fresh curly parsley

50ml (2fl oz) claret (full bodied red wine)

1 tsp Worcestershire sauce

1 bay leaf

salt and freshly ground black pepper

FOR THE SUET PASTRY

175g (6oz) beef or vegetarian suet

350g (12oz) self-raising flour, plus extra for dusting

¼ tsp ground turmeric

about 225ml (8fl oz) cold water

. . . .

Serves 4

BEEF PIE WITH A CRISPY POTATO CRUST

This is British food at its best. What could be nicer than a plate of steaming beef pie on a cold winter's day? The potato topping is slightly more tricky to make than regular mash, but worth it. Crispy on the outside, soft and buttery inside, your guests will be begging for the recipe. Use Golden Wonder, Cyprus or another starchy potato for the best results.

350g (12oz) potatoes, as even-sized
   as possible
3 tbsp olive oil
55g (2oz) butter
800g (1lb 12oz) chuck beef steak,
   trimmed and cut into 5cm
   (2 inch) cubes
3 large onions, thinly sliced
1 tsp chopped fresh thyme
2 tbsp plain flour
600ml (1 pint) stout
300ml (½ pint) beef stock
1 tsp light muscovado sugar
1 tbsp red wine vinegar
25g (1oz) butter
salt and freshly ground black pepper

. . . .

Serves 4–6

Preheat the oven to 170C/325F/Gas 3. Cook the potatoes in a large pan of boiling salted water. Bring to the boil, then reduce the heat and simmer for 10 minutes until the potatoes are just starting to soften but are not cooked through. Drain, then quickly cool under cold running water before coarsely grating. Set aside until needed.

Meanwhile, heat a heavy-based pan. Add the oil and butter and, as soon as it starts smoking, tip in the beef. Quickly brown on all sides, then transfer to a plate with a slotted spoon. Set aside.

Add the onions to the pan and cook for a few minutes until lightly browned, stirring occasionally. Stir in the thyme and then spoon into a bowl and set aside. Stir the flour into the remaining fat in the pan and cook over a low heat, stirring constantly, until you have a dark gold roux .

Gradually pour in the stout, stirring until smooth after each addition. Pour in the stock, stirring to combine, and season to taste, then add the sugar and vinegar. Bring to the boil, stirring constantly, and then simmer gently for 15 minutes until thickened and slightly reduced.

Tip the reserved beef and onions into an ovenproof dish and mix well. Strain over the sauce through a fine sieve. Cover tightly with foil and cook for 3 hours until the beef is completely tender and the liquid has reduced and thickened.

Increase the oven temperature to 190C/375F/Gas 5. Sprinkle the reserved grated potato over the meat and onion mixture and dot with the butter. Return the pie to the oven for 30 minutes until the potato crust is nice and crispy. Serve immediately.

TAGLIATELLE WITH BOLOGNESE SAUCE

I love this dish and it's one of many recipes in Italy where dried pasta is actually the best option. It supplies a good, *al dente* texture that is impossible to achieve with fresh pasta. When buying dried pasta, always choose one from a traditional Italian manufacturer.

Place the minced pork in a bowl with the minced beef and two tablespoons of the olive oil. Mix together until well combined.

Heat the remaining olive oil in a large pan with a lid. Add the onion and celery and cook for 5 minutes, stirring occasionally, until softened but not coloured, .

Gradually add the meat mixture to the onion and celery, stirring all the time to break down any lumps.

Increase the heat, add the red wine and simmer until the liquid has reduced by half. Stir in the tomato purée and chicken stock, then lower the heat and throw in the rosemary sprigs.

Cover the pan and leave to cook on a low heat for 2–2½ hours until you have achieved a rich, thick sauce and the beef is meltingly tender. Season to taste.

When ready to eat, bring a large pan of water to a rolling boil. Add a good pinch of salt, then add the tagliatelle and cook for 6–8 minutes or according to packet instructions until the pasta is *al dente*. Drain and quickly refresh under cold running water, then return to the pan and add a good drizzle of olive oil.

Divide the tagliatelle between warm bowls and spoon over the Bolognese sauce. Sprinkle over the pecorino shavings to serve.

250g (9oz) good quality minced pork
250g (9oz) good quality minced beef
6 tbsp olive oil, plus extra for drizzling
1 onion, very finely chopped
1 celery stick, very finely chopped
250ml (9fl oz) red wine
4 tbsp tomato purée
1.2 litres (2 pints) chicken stock
2 fresh rosemary sprigs
300g (10½ oz) tagliatelle
salt and freshly ground black pepper
pecorino shavings, to garnish

....

Serves 4

MONGOLIAN BEEF

This delicious dish originates from northern China and promotes health and well-being. It is unusual to use minced beef as I've suggested here, but I think it gives a lovely light texture and holds the flavour of the spices really well.

600g (1lb 5oz) good quality minced beef

1 head Chinese cabbage, halved, tough core removed and finely shredded

2 tsp sea salt

50ml (2fl oz) vegetable oil

2 tbsp rice wine

2 tbsp hoisin sauce

1 tbsp oyster sauce

1 tsp malt vinegar

1/2 tsp toasted sesame oil

1 small carrot, finely sliced

1 small red pepper, halved, cored and finely sliced

1 bunch spring onions, trimmed and finely sliced

steamed rice and sliced fresh green and red chillies, to serve

FOR THE MARINADE

2 tbsp rice wine

1 tbsp light soy sauce

1 tbsp cornflour

1 tbsp finely diced fresh root ginger

1 tbsp finely diced garlic

1/2 tsp toasted sesame oil

....

Serves 4

To make the marinade, place the rice wine in a shallow non-metallic dish and add the light soy sauce, cornflour, ginger, garlic and sesame oil. Stir in the minced beef until well combined, then cover with cling film and leave to marinate in the fridge for 30 minutes.

Place the cabbage in a bowl with the salt and stir well, then leave to stand for 15 minutes. Tip into a colander and rinse well under cold running water and leave to drain. Squeeze out any excess water with your hands. Set aside.

Heat a wok until smoking hot. Add two tablespoons of oil, swirling it up the sides and once the surface of the wok starts to shimmer slightly tip in half of the marinated beef and stir fry for 30 seconds, breaking up any lumps with a wooden spoon. Transfer the cooked minced beef to a bowl with a slotted spoon and set aside.

Add the remaining oil to the wok and stir fry the rest of the beef for 30 seconds, again breaking up any lumps with a wooden spoon. Return the reserved cooked minced beef to the wok with the rice wine, hoisin and oyster sauce, vinegar and sesame oil and stir fry for another 30 seconds. Toss in the reserved cabbage with the carrot and pepper and stir fry for another minute until just tender but still crisp. Stir in the spring onions, reserving a few to garnish and remove from the heat.

Spoon the beef into warmed bowls and sprinkle over the remaining spring onions. Serve with separate bowls of rice and sliced chillies and let everyone help themselves.

STIR-FRIED BEEF

This is a great dish because it's so quick, easy and delicious. The combination of flavours turns the beef strips into a gourmet delight. When served with noodles, it becomes the type of wholesome, satisfying meal that is the hallmark of the best of Chinese home cooking.

450g (1lb) rump steak, trimmed and cut into strips
3 tbsp groundnut oil
225g (8oz) egg noodles
225g (8oz) onions, coarsely chopped
4 garlic cloves, coarsely chopped
100ml (3½ fl oz) beef stock
115g (4oz) button mushrooms, sliced
1 tsp dried chilli flakes
pinch caster sugar
1 tbsp soy sauce
2 large gherkins, sliced
handful fresh chives, trimmed and snipped in half
2 tsp toasted sesame oil

FOR THE MARINADE
2 tbsp soy sauce
1 tsp toasted sesame oil
1 tbsp cornflour, mixed with a little water to make a paste

. . . .

Serves 4

To make the marinade, place the soy sauce in a shallow non-metallic dish with the sesame oil and cornflour paste. Mix well to combine and then add the beef. Leave for about 20 minutes, covered, if time allows.

Heat a wok or large frying pan over a high heat until it's very hot. Add the oil and, when it's slightly smoking, remove the beef from the marinade with a slotted spoon and add it to the wok. Stir fry for 2 minutes until it's barely cooked. Transfer to a colander or sieve with a slotted spoon and leave to drain off the excess oil.

Cook the egg noodles in a pan of boiling water for 3–5 minutes until tender. Drain off all but about 1 tablespoon of oil from the wok and re-heat. Add the onions and garlic and stir fry for 2 minutes. Add the beef stock and mushrooms and continue to cook for 3 minutes until the onions have softened and the mushrooms are tender.

Add the chilli flakes, sugar and soy sauce and cook for another minute. Stir in the gherkins and then return the beef to the pan and continue to cook until warmed through. Sprinkle over the chives and half the sesame oil, then give the mixture a few stirs. Drain the egg noodles and toss in the remaining sesame oil.

Arrange the noodles on warmed plates with the stir-fried beef to serve.

THAI BEEF SALAD

ANTONY WORRALL THOMPSON

Look out for rice noodles that are opaque white in colour and come in a variety of shapes. One of the most common are rice stick noodles, which are flat and about the length of a chopstick. They can vary in thickness but make a perfect vehicle for this salad.

To make the marinade, mix together the light muscovado sugar, soy sauce and sesame oil in a shallow non-metallic dish. Add the beef, then cover with cling film and leave to marinate for up to 1 hour, turning occasionally.

Soak the rice noodles in a bowl of warm water for 25 minutes or according to packet instructions, then drain them in a colander or sieve.

Heat a heavy-based frying pan until hot. Add a little sunflower oil and carefully swirl it around to coat the base with a very thin film. Add the marinated steaks, reserving any remaining marinade. Sear for 1 minute on each side.

Remove the steaks from the pan and thinly slice, then return to the pan with the remaining marinade and cook for another minute or two. Scatter over most of the coriander, reserving a little to garnish, and mix well. Transfer the beef to a plate with a slotted spoon and continue to reduce the marinade until you have a nice sauce consistency.

Mix together the lime juice, fish sauce, chilli flakes and caster sugar in a small bowl. Tip the prepared noodles into a large bowl and add the basil, mint and spring onions. Add the lime juice mixture and toss until well combined.

Pile the noodle mixture onto a platter and spoon the beef slices on top. Drizzle over the sauce and scatter the rest of the coriander on top to serve.

4 x 115g (4oz) fillet steaks
225g (8oz) rice noodles
sunflower oil, for cooking
4 tbsp fresh coriander, roughly chopped
juice of 2 limes
2 tbsp Thai fish sauce (nam pla)
1 tsp dried chilli flakes
1 tsp caster sugar
handful fresh basil leaves, roughly torn
handful fresh mint leaves, finely chopped
1 bunch spring onions, trimmed and roughly chopped

FOR THE MARINADE
4 tbsp light muscovado sugar
4 tbsp soy sauce
4 tsp toasted sesame oil

Serves 4

pork

BRAISED PORK BELLY WITH BOULANGERE POTATOES

I adore this inexpensive cut of pork and like to serve it very simply. At first glance it might look rather fatty but the majority of the fat should be cooked off at the beginning when sealing in the pan. Just make sure that you remove all traces of fat from the sauce before reducing it.

Preheat the oven to 180C/350F/Gas 4. Heat a heavy, cast iron pan over a high heat. Season the pork belly and place in the pan, fat side down. Cook for a few minutes until golden, then quickly sear on all sides to seal. Remove from the heat and leave to rest for about 5 minutes.

Pour the cider into a large jug and crumble in the beef stock cube. Stir in the sugar and add the star anise and fennel seeds. Season lightly and set aside.

Place the onion in a roasting tin with the garlic and thyme, tossing to mix. Put the pork belly on top and pour in the cider mixture. Braise the pork belly for 1½ hours until tender.

Peel the potatoes and slice them very thinly using a mandolin or slicing attachment on a food processor. Slice the onions in the same manner. Melt 40g (1½oz) of the butter in a pan and sweat the onions for 5 minutes until soft but not coloured.

Butter an ovenproof dish. Layer up the sliced potatoes, cabbage and sweated onions, sprinkling with the thyme and seasoning to taste in between each layer. Finish with a neat layer of overlapping potato slices and then press down firmly using the palms of your hands.

Bring the stock to a simmer in a small pan and pour over the potato layers. Dot the rest of the butter on top. Cover with foil and bake for 1 hour in the oven with the pork until the potatoes are cooked through and tender. Remove the foil and return to the oven for 10 minutes until golden brown.

When the pork belly is cooked, transfer to a warm plate and leave to rest for at least 20 minutes. To make the sauce, strain the remaining liquor into a clean pan and reduce until you have a good syrupy consistency.

Carve the rested pork belly into slices and arrange on plates with the boulangère potatoes. Pour over a little sauce to serve.

1.5kg (3lb 5oz) pork belly, rind removed
1 litre (1¾ pints) good quality dry cider
1 beef stock cube
125g (4½ oz) golden caster sugar
1 star anise
5 fennel seeds, lightly crushed
1 onion, sliced
4 garlic cloves, sliced
4 fresh thyme sprigs
salt and freshly ground black pepper

FOR THE BOULANGERE POTATOES
1kg (2lb 4oz) floury potatoes, such as Maris Piper
2 onions, peeled
85g (3oz) butter
115g (4oz) Savoy cabbage, finely shredded
400ml (14fl oz) chicken or vegetable stock
¼ tsp fresh thyme leaves

. . . .

Serves 4–6

SLOW-ROAST PORK WITH SPICED PINEAPPLE SALSA

For those of you who think you haven't got time to prepare a wonderful joint, then think again. This recipe takes no more than ten minutes to prepare and then it can just be left to cook. The end result is a fantastic taste sensation. Get your butcher to score the pork skin as it can be tricky to do yourself unless you have a very sharp knife or Stanley blade.

4 garlic cloves, crushed
1 tbsp freshly grated root ginger
1 tbsp Maldon sea salt
2 tbsp jerk seasoning
1 tbsp light muscovado sugar
1–2 tbsp dark rum (optional)
1 tbsp olive oil
3kg (6lb 8oz) boned and rolled shoulder
   of pork, rind scored
125ml (4fl oz) dry white wine
salt and freshly ground black pepper

FOR THE PINEAPPLE SALSA
1 ripe pineapple
1 tbsp caster sugar
½ large red chilli, seeded and
   finely chopped
2 tsp freshly grated root ginger
finely grated rind and juice of 1 lime
   (unwaxed if possible)
1 small red onion, finely chopped
1 tbsp chopped fresh mint
1 tbsp chopped fresh coriander

. . . .

Serves 6–8

Preheat the oven to 230C/450F/Gas 8. Place the garlic, ginger, sea salt, jerk seasoning, sugar, rum (if using) and oil in a pestle and mortar and crush to make a paste. Using your hands, rub this mixture into the pork rind, pushing it well into the slits. Place the pork, rind-side up, on a rack in a large roasting tin and roast in the middle shelf of the hot oven for 30 minutes.

Remove the pork from the oven and turn the temperature down to 150C/250F/Gas 2. Turn the pork over so that the rind is on the bottom and return to the oven to cook very slowly for at least 5–6 hours. Halfway through, pour 225ml (8fl oz) water into the roasting tin, turn the pork rind-side up again, baste with the juices in the tin and continue to cook.

To make the salsa, peel and core the pineapple. Dice the flesh into 1cm (½ inch) cubes and mix with the sugar. Heat a non-stick frying pan over a high heat, add the pineapple and cook quickly for about 2 minutes to caramelize lightly. Tip into a bowl, add the chilli, ginger, lime rind and juice, onion and herbs. Season to taste and set aside for at least 30 minutes to allow the flavours to develop.

About 45 minutes before serving, turn the oven up to 220C/425F/Gas 7. Transfer the pork to a clean roasting tin and cook for about 20 minutes to crisp up the rind. Keep an eye on the meat to make sure the rind crackles rather than burns. Once cooked through, remove from the oven and leave to rest in a warm place for 20 minutes.

While the pork is resting, make the gravy. Spoon off any excess fat from the first roasting tin, add the white wine and place over a low heat. Slowly bring to the boil, stirring well to incorporate any bits from the bottom of the tin. Simmer for a couple of minutes, season and strain into a jug.

Cut the pork into thick slices and arrange on warmed plates. Serve with the bowl of pineapple salsa and jug of gravy.

FAST BARBECUED RIBS

There are very few things that are as much fun to eat as spare ribs. Juicy and bursting with flavour they are fairly easy to prepare if you use this method. The ribs are first cooked in a low oven for 1 hour to render some of the fat and to tenderize them at the same time. This can be done up to 4 hours in advance.

Preheat the oven to 150C/300F/Gas 2. Place the pork ribs in a large roasting tin and sprinkle evenly with the salt and pepper. Put in the oven and roast for 1 hour, then take out. This can be up to 4 hours in advance.

To make the barbecue sauce, pour the hoisin sauce into a food processor or liquidizer with the sesame oil, light soy sauce, Thai fish sauce, rice wine or dry sherry, garlic, ginger, chilli-bean sauce and sugar. Whizz until well blended.

Preheat the grill to high or make a charcoal fire in the barbecue. When the grill is very hot or the charcoal is ash-white, baste the ribs on both sides with the barbecue sauce and then cook on a grill rack for 10 minutes on each side, until cooked all the way through.

Transfer the ribs to a warmed platter to serve.

1.5kg (3lb 5oz) pork spare ribs

2 tsp salt

1 tsp freshly ground five pepper (or use black pepper)

FOR THE BARBECUE SAUCE

5 tbsp hoisin sauce

3 tbsp toasted sesame oil

2 tbsp light soy sauce

2 tbsp Thai fish sauce (nam pla)

2 tbsp Shaoxing rice wine or dry sherry

3 tbsp coarsely chopped garlic

2 tsp finely chopped fresh root ginger

2 tbsp chilli-bean sauce

2 tsp caster sugar

. . . .

Serves 4–6

THYME-ROASTED PORK CHOPS WITH PUY LENTIL RAGOUT AND CIDER MUSTARD SAUCE

This dish is magnificent and so easy, but it does need the very best loin pork chops. Swaddles Green farm have a good selection of old British breeds, reared slowly for unforced growth. All their pork is from free-range Saddleback, Berkshire and Large Black pigs. They run an excellent mail order service so their pork is easy to get hold of.

4 thick cut pork chops (preferably organic)
2 tbsp olive oil
¼ tsp fresh thyme leaves
salt and freshly ground black pepper

FOR THE CIDER SAUCE
100ml (3½ fl oz) chicken stock
100ml (3½ fl oz) cider
100ml (3½ fl oz) double cream
50ml (2fl oz) calvados
2 tbsp wholegrain mustard

FOR THE LENTIL RAGOUT
400ml (14fl oz) good quality chicken stock
200g (7oz) Puy lentils
1 tbsp olive oil
115g (4oz) onion, finely chopped
115g (4oz) celery, finely chopped
115g (4oz) carrot, finely chopped
115g (4oz) smoked bacon lardons
2 garlic cloves, finely chopped
½ Savoy cabbage, thick core removed and finely shredded
1 tbsp chopped fresh flat-leaf parsley

. . . .

Serves 4

Preheat the oven to 180C/350F/Gas 4. Heat an ovenproof frying pan. Rub the pork chops all over with the olive oil, thyme and seasoning and then put into the pan. Cook for 3 minutes until coloured, then turn over and place in the oven for 15 minutes until the pork is completely tender and cooked through. Remove from the oven and leave to rest for 5 minutes.

To make the Puy lentil ragout, pour the chicken stock into a pan and bring to the boil. Add the lentils and simmer for about 20 minutes or until the lentils are *al dente* and all of the stock has been absorbed.

Meanwhile, heat the oil in a large frying pan. Add the onion, celery, carrot and bacon and sauté for 10 minutes until the bacon is crisp and the vegetables have softened. Stir in the garlic and cabbage and continue to cook for another couple of minutes until the cabbage has wilted and is tender. Fold in the cooked lentils with the parsley and season to taste. Keep warm.

To make the sauce, place the stock in a pan with the cider, cream, calvados and mustard. Bring to the boil, give it a good stir, then reduce the heat and simmer for about 5 minutes until well reduced and thickened to a nice sauce consistency. Season to taste.

Divide the Puy lentil ragout among warmed wide-rimmed bowls or plates. Slice each chop in two and arrange on top, then spoon around the cider mustard sauce to serve.

ORIENTAL PORK CHOPS WITH PICKLED CHINESE SALAD

The wonderful flavours in these pork chops make them perfect barbecue food with a twist, particularly when served with the pickled Chinese salad. The marinade could also be used with great success on slashed chicken fillets or rib-eye steaks.

4 x 225g (8oz) thick cut pork chops
salt and freshly ground black pepper
steamed rice, to serve

FOR THE PICKLED SALAD
2 red chillies, seeded and
 finely chopped
2 tbsp mirin
2 tbsp light soy sauce
1 tbsp caster sugar
1 cucumber, thinly sliced using a
 vegetable peeler
4 small carrots, thinly sliced using a
 vegetable peeler
1 Chinese cabbage, halved, cored
 and shredded

FOR THE MARINADE
3 large red chillies, seeded and chopped
4 large garlic cloves, chopped
1 tsp freshly grated root ginger
2 tbsp Thai fish sauce (nam pla)
1 tsp light muscovado sugar
juice of 1 lime
2 tbsp light soy sauce
2 tbsp mirin (rice wine)
2 tbsp groundnut oil
2 tbsp chopped fresh basil
2 tbsp chopped fresh coriander

To make the marinade, place the chillies in a food processor or liquidizer with the garlic, ginger, fish sauce, sugar, lime juice, light soy sauce, mirin, oil and herbs. Blitz until smooth and carefully pour into a large zip lock bag. Season the pork chops all over and then add to the bag. Place in the fridge to marinate for at least 2 hours or up to 24 hours is better. Remove from the fridge and allow to come back to room temperature before you cook them.

Preheat the oven to 200C/400F/Gas 6. Transfer the marinated pork chops from the zip-lock bag with about four spoonfuls of the marinade to a roasting tin. Roast for 20-25 minutes, basting occasionally, until the pork chops are completely tender and just catching around the edges.

Place the remaining marinade in a small pan and boil for 5–10 minutes until well reduced and sticky. Keep the sauce warm until needed.

To make the salad, mix the chillies in a bowl with the mirin, light soy sauce and caster sugar. Put the cucumber in a large bowl with the carrots and Chinese cabbage. Fold in the chilli dressing and cover with cling film. Leave in the fridge for up to 1 hour to allow the dressing to pickle the vegetables.

Place some steamed rice in each warmed bowl and top with an Oriental pork chop. Drizzle over some of the sauce and serve with the pickled salad.

Serves 4

THAI RED PORK CURRY WITH COCONUT RICE

If you like Thai green chicken curry, then you are going to like this dish. Make it as hot or as mild as you like by adjusting the quantity of curry paste. Feel free to substitute the pork with skinless, boneless chicken or duck fillets.

To make the coconut rice, put the rice in a large bowl and wash it several times until the water becomes clear. Drain well and place in a heavy-based pan with a tight-fitting lid. Add the coconut milk, salt and sugar with 300ml (½ pint) of water. Bring to a simmer, then turn the heat down as low as possible. Cover and leave to cook undisturbed for 15 minutes. Remove from the heat and leave to stand covered for another 10 minutes until all of the liquid has been absorbed and the rice is tender.

Heat a wok or large frying pan over a medium heat and pour in the oil. Add the curry paste and stir fry for 30 seconds. Add the pork slices, increase the heat and stir fry for 1 minute. Remove with a slotted spoon to a colander or sieve and set to one side, allowing any excess fat to drain off.

Add the ginger to the wok with the turmeric and garlic and stir fry for 10 seconds. Stir in the coconut milk, fish sauce, kaffir lime leaves and sugar and bring to the boil. Reduce the heat and simmer for 5 minutes. Return the pork to the pan and simmer for 3 minutes until the pork is cooked through. Stir through the basil.

Divide the coconut rice among warmed bowls and spoon the Thai red pork curry on top to serve.

1½ tbsp vegetable oil
2 tbsp Thai red curry paste
450g (1lb) pork fillet, cut into thin slices
3 tbsp finely shredded fresh root ginger
1 tsp ground turmeric
2 tbsp finely sliced garlic
400g can coconut milk
2 tbsp Thai fish sauce (nam pla)
4 kaffir lime leaves
2 tsp caster sugar
handful fresh basil leaves, roughly torn

FOR THE COCONUT RICE
400g (14oz) long grain white rice
400g can coconut milk
½ tsp salt
1 tsp sugar

. . . .

Serves 4

CHAR SIU PORK WITH STEAMED PAK CHOI

Char siu served in Chinese restaurants is reddish brown due to the use of colouring, but if you're making it yourself at home you can omit it. When roasted for a sufficient time the char siu becomes a gorgeous golden brown colour on the edges. The key to success is not to overcook the pork so that the meat remains succulent.

Cut slashes into the pork fillet. Place the garlic in a shallow non-metallic dish and add the ginger, soy sauce, rice wine, sugar, hoisin sauce, yellow bean sauce, vegetable oil and honey. Mix well and add the pork, turning to coat. Cover with cling film and leave to marinate in the fridge for at least 2 hours or up to 24 hours is better, turning occasionally. Remove from the fridge and allow to come back to room temperature before you cook it.

Preheat the oven to 200C/400F/Gas 6. Remove the pork from the marinade and place on a rack set over a roasting tin, reserving the rest of the marinade. Pour in enough hot water to come halfway up the sides of the tin. Roast for 20 minutes.

Reduce the oven temperature to 180C/350F/Gas 4. Turn the pork fillet over and brush over some of the remaining marinade. Roast for another 20 minutes until the pork is completely tender and lightly glazed. Cover the cooked char sui pork with foil and leave to rest for 5 minutes in a warm place.

Place the remaining marinade in a small pan and simmer for a few minutes until you have a sauce-like consistency. Season to taste.

Place the baby pak choi in a steamer and cook for 3–4 minutes or until tender. Slice vertically.

Carve the rested char siu pork into slices and arrange on warmed plates with the steamed pak choi. Drizzle over the sauce and sprinkle over the spring onion. Serve at once.

500g (1lb 2oz) pork fillet (in one piece)
200g (7oz) baby pak choi, left whole
1 spring onion, finely sliced
salt and freshly ground black pepper

FOR THE MARINADE
2 garlic cloves, crushed
2 tbsp freshly grated root ginger
50ml (2fl oz) light soy sauce
50ml (2fl oz) rice wine
3 tbsp light muscovado sugar
1 tbsp hoisin sauce
2 tbsp yellow bean sauce
1 tbsp vegetable oil
4 tbsp clear honey

· ·

Serves 2–3

PORK AND CARAMELIZED PEAR PIE WITH CUCUMBER AND MUSTARD SEED RELISH

This homely supper dish is guaranteed to make all the family swoon but it will only be as good as the raw ingredients that you use. I was lucky enough to be able to use some superb free-range pork from a place called Caherbeg in West Cork, but it's worth making a trip to your local farmers' market to see what they have on offer.

50g (2oz) butter

200g (7oz) pears, peeled, quartered and cored

2 tbsp clear honey

400g (14oz) pork sausagemeat (preferably free-range)

200g (7oz) rindless streaky bacon, diced

1 tbsp fresh thyme, roughly chopped

300g (10 1/2 oz) puff pastry, thawed if frozen

a little plain flour, for dusting

1 egg, beaten

salt and freshly ground black pepper

lightly dressed green salad, to serve

FOR THE RELISH

1/2 cucumber

1 onion, peeled

225g (8oz) caster sugar

2 tsp brown mustard seeds

150ml (1/4 pint) cider vinegar

....

Serves 6

To make the relish, using a mandolin thinly slice the cucumber and onion into a large bowl. Sprinkle over the sugar, mustard seeds, vinegar and one teaspoon of salt. Cover with a clean towel and set aside for about 2 hours. Then give the cucumber pickle a good stir and leave for another hour. This can be kept covered in the fridge or in a sterilized jar.

Preheat the oven to 160C/320F/Gas 2. Melt the butter in a frying pan over a medium heat. Add the pears and honey and cook for 10 minutes, tossing frequently, until caramelized.

Butter a casserole dish and then scatter in a third of the sausage meat with a third of the bacon. Season to taste and then sprinkle over the thyme. Scatter over a third of the caramelized pears, then repeat the layers until all the ingredients are used up and you have reached the top of the casserole dish.

On a lightly floured board or work surface, roll out the pastry until it's large enough to cover the top of the casserole dish. Use to cover the pie, pushing down the edges to form a seal. Prick the top with a fork and then brush with beaten egg. Bake for 55–60 minutes until the pastry is puffed up and has turned a lovely golden colour and the filling is cooked through.

Cut generous slices of the pie and arrange on warmed plates with some of the cucumber and mustard seed relish. Serve with a bowl of lightly dressed green salad.

CRISPY BACON, PEA AND GARLIC CREAM PASTA

This makes a nice change from your average bowl of pasta and is perfect for the nights when you don't have a lot in the fridge but want something tasty. The garlic cream cheese thinned down with a little cream makes an instant rich and creamy sauce and would also work with strips of smoked salmon and freshly grated Parmesan or broccoli florets with cubes of cooked chicken, depending on what you have.

350g (12oz) pasta, such as trompetti
   or penne
225g (8oz) rindless bacon rashers
115g (4oz) garlic cream cheese,
   such as Boursin
150ml (¼ pint) single cream
115g (4oz) frozen peas, defrosted
a little olive oil
salt and freshly ground black pepper

. . . .

Serves 4

Cook the pasta in a pan of boiling salted water for 8–10 minutes or according to packet instructions, until *al dente* .

Preheat the grill and arrange the bacon on a grill rack. Cook for a few minutes on each side until crisp. Transfer to kitchen paper to drain and then snip into small pieces with a pair of scissors.

Meanwhile, melt the cream cheese in a small pan with the cream, stirring until smooth. Stir in the peas and cooked bacon pieces and then allow to warm through. Season to taste.

Drain the cooked pasta and return to the pan, then drizzle over a little olive oil to keep it from sticking together. Pour over the crispy bacon, pea and cream cheese mixture. Season to taste and then mix together until evenly combined.

Divide between warm wide-rimmed bowls and serve at once.

MARMALADE AND MUSTARD BAKED HAM WITH BROCCOLI BAKE

I've been making this recipe for a very long time. It's old fashioned and a touch too heavy on the calories but completely delicious. To cut down on its gut-bursting properties, serve it with a sharp green salad. If you are not a fan of broccoli try using thickly sliced leeks with cauliflower or Brussels sprouts instead.

Soak the gammon in cold water overnight, then rinse well and place in a large pan with a lid. Cover with fresh cold water. Add the onion, carrot, bay leaves and peppercorns. Slowly bring to the boil, then cover and simmer very gently for 1 hour and 30 minutes until just cooked through and tender. Remove from the heat and leave in its liquid to cool for 30–40 minutes.

Preheat the oven to 200C/400F/Gas 6. Remove the gammon joint from the cooking liquid and carefully cut away the rind and some of the excess fat. Cut the remaining fat in a lattice pattern and place in a small roasting tin. Pour in the orange juice and then arrange the orange slices on the gammon joint securing them in place with the cloves.

Mix together the mustard, marmalade and sugar in a small bowl. Season generously with pepper and then smear all over the gammon joint. Bake for 25–30 minutes or until the orange slices are lightly browned and caramelized and the meat is cooked through. Remove from the oven and leave to rest in a warm place for at least 20 minutes.

Meanwhile, prepare the broccoli bake. Preheat the grill. Cook the broccoli in a pan of boiling salted water for 3 minutes until just cooked through. Drain well and tip into a baking dish. Dollop over the crème fraîche and season to taste, then sprinkle the Cheddar and Parmesan on top. Place under the grill for 10 minutes until bubbling and golden brown.

Carve the ham into slices and arrange on warmed plates. Place the broccoli bake on the table and let everyone help themselves.

1.75kg (3lb 14oz) gammon joint
1 onion, roughly chopped
1 carrot, roughly chopped
2 bay leaves
12 black peppercorns
200ml (7fl oz) freshly squeezed orange juice
2 oranges, finely sliced and pips removed
handful of whole cloves
2 tbsp wholegrain mustard
2 tbsp marmalade
2 tbsp light muscovado sugar
salt and freshly ground black pepper

FOR THE BROCCOLI BAKE
500g (1lb 2oz) broccoli, cut into florets
350ml (12fl oz) crème fraîche
25g (1oz) Cheddar, grated
25g (1oz) freshly grated Parmesan

. . . .

Serves 4–6

lamb

MUSTARD AND HERB CRUSTED BEST END OF LAMB WITH BRAISED VEGETABLES

British lamb is fantastic, especially if you go to the trouble of tracking down some of the native breeds that many butchers and some of the supermarkets are now stocking. This dish is perfect for serving from the end of May until mid-September when there is plenty of spring lamb available.

2 x 7-bone best end of lamb

2 tbsp olive oil

55g (2oz) fresh white breadcrumbs

4 fresh rosemary sprigs, leaves stripped and finely chopped

2 tbsp Dijon mustard

25g (1oz) butter

1 tsp tomato purée

75ml (2 ½ fl oz) red wine

200ml (7fl oz) lamb stock

salt and freshly ground black pepper

FOR THE BRAISED VEGETABLES

2 carrots, chopped lengthways

150g (5 ½ oz) new potatoes, scrubbed and chopped

55g (2oz) baby turnips, scrubbed and chopped

50g (1 ¾ oz) lentils

55g (2oz) butter

1 tbsp caster sugar

bunch fresh mint, leaves stripped and chopped

3 tbsp red wine vinegar

. . . .

Serves 4–6

Preheat the oven to 180C/350F/Gas 4 and heat a heavy-based pan. Trim any excess fat from the lamb and cut into two equal sized pieces. Add the oil to the pan and then quickly sear the two pieces of lamb to seal in the juices.

Mix the breadcrumbs and rosemary on a flat plate. Brush the fat side of the sealed lamb with the mustard and then roll it in the breadcrumb mixture to create a crust. Arrange side-by-side in a roasting tin and roast for 25 minutes for pink lamb or longer if you prefer your meat well-done. When the lamb is cooked, transfer to a warm dish and leave to rest in a warm place for about 15 minutes.

Meanwhile, prepare the braised vegetables. Place the carrots in a large pan with the new potatoes and baby turnips. Tip in the lentils and pour in 300ml (½ pint) of water. Add the butter and sugar and bring to the boil, then boil fast for 20–25 minutes or until all of the vegetables and lentils are tender and the water has evaporated. Stir in the mint and red wine vinegar and cook for another few minutes to combine, stirring occasionally. Season to taste.

To make the gravy, heat the butter and tomato purée for 1 minute in a small pan. Add the red wine and cook for a few minutes or until reduced to a fifth of the original quantity. Pour in the stock and again reduce for about 5 minutes or until reduced to a fifth of the original quantity. Season to taste.

Carve the lamb into individual cutlets. Spoon the braised vegetables onto warmed plates and arrange the lamb cutlets on top. Drizzle around the gravy to serve.

RACK OF LAMB WITH PISTACHIO CRUST

Spring is the time of year when British products start to come into their own: wonderful new season lamb served with English asparagus and the first crop of potatoes. Foods seem to taste so much better when eaten in their true seasons. Ask your butcher to French trim the racks of lamb for you.

2 x 7-bone best ends of lamb, each about 280–350g (10–12oz)
about 1 tbsp prepared English mustard
salt and freshly ground black pepper
steamed asparagus and boiled new potatoes, to serve

FOR THE PISTACHIO CRUST
55g (2oz) unsalted butter
55g (2oz) shelled pistachio nuts
2 tbsp fresh soft thyme leaves
2 tbsp snipped fresh chives
2 tbsp chopped fresh flat-leaf parsley
55g (2oz) fresh white breadcrumbs
finely grated rind of 1/2 lemon
1 small garlic clove, roughly chopped

....

Serves 4

To make the pistachio crust, melt the butter in a small pan or in the microwave. Place in a food processor with the pistachio nuts, thyme leaves, chives and parsley and blitz until bright green. Add the breadcrumbs, lemon rind, garlic and some seasoning and blend again for just a few seconds until all the ingredients are well combined.

Place the racks of lamb on a chopping board and using a pastry brush spread the mustard thickly over the fat side of each rack. Cover with the pistachio crumbs, using your hands to mould it over the lamb. Arrange the lamb, coated side up, on a baking sheet and chill for at least 30 minutes or up to 2 hours to allow the crust to 'set'. Allow the meat to return to room temperature before cooking.

Preheat the oven to 200C/400F/Gas 6. Place the racks of lamb in a small roasting tin and roast for 20–25 minutes, or a little longer depending on how well-done you like your lamb. Remove the lamb from the oven and set aside in a warm place to rest for 10–15 minutes.

Carve the lamb into chops and serve on warmed plates with the steamed asparagus and new potatoes.

RUMP OF WELSH LAMB WITH BROAD BEANS AND CHERRY TOMATOES

For me, there's nothing nicer for a romantic dinner than some succulent new season lamb, garnished with roasted cherry tomatoes and broad beans – delicious. I always choose Welsh lamb, as I am confident of the traceability from farm to plate.

Preheat the oven to 220C/425F/Gas 7. Heat a large ovenproof frying pan, then add the olive oil and allow to heat through. Season the lamb rump and add to the hot pan, then sear all over until well sealed and golden brown.

Add the shallots to the pan with the rosemary, garlic and cherry tomatoes, tossing gently. Put in the oven and roast for 20–25 minutes until the lamb is just tender but still slightly pink in the middle; cook for longer if you prefer your meat more well done.

Meanwhile, place the chicken stock in a small pan and reduce by half. Set aside. Blanch the broad beans in a pan of boiling water for 1–2 minutes, then drain and when cool enough to handle slip off the skins. Set aside.

Transfer the lamb, shallots and tomatoes to a plate and leave to rest in a warm place for 10–15 minutes. Just before you are ready to serve, place the roasting tin directly on the hob to heat. Add the reduced chicken stock and blanched beans to the pan that the lamb and vegetables were in and simmer for 1–2 minutes until the beans are warmed through, stirring with a wooden spoon to release any sediment from the bottom of the pan. Season to taste.

Carve the lamb into thick slices and arrange on plates with the cherry tomatoes and shallots. Drizzle the broad beans and sauce over the top to serve.

1 tbsp olive oil

400g (14oz) new season Welsh rump of lamb, trimmed

4 banana shallots, unpeeled and cut in half

4 fresh rosemary sprigs, soaked in cold water

6 garlic cloves, unpeeled and soaked in cold water

4 bunches cherry tomatoes on the vine (with about 5 tomatoes per stem)

200ml (7fl oz) chicken stock

300g (10½ oz) broad beans

salt and freshly ground black pepper

. . . .

Serves 2

LEG OF LAMB WRAPPED IN ROSEMARY

Ask your butcher to remove the hip joint from a leg of lamb. For perfect results every time make sure you dry off the lamb before roasting, it makes all the difference to the flavour. Allowing the lamb to rest for one-third of the time it has taken to cook ensures perfectly pink meat.

1 leg of lamb, hip joint removed, about 2kg (4lb 8oz) in total
4 garlic cloves, cut into slivers
6 anchovy fillets, quartered
2 tbsp olive oil
10–12 sprigs fresh rosemary
100g (3 1/2 oz) black olive paste (or pitted kalamata olives, puréed)
juice of 1/2 lemon, pips removed
salt and freshly ground black pepper

. . . .

Serves 4–6

Dry the lamb well until its surface is dry to the touch. Trim off and discard any excess fat. Make incisions all over the meat using a small sharp knife, creating little pockets roughly one knuckle deep; that's about 4cm (1½ inches). Push a garlic sliver and a piece of anchovy into each incision, then season all over with pepper.

Heat half of the oil in a flameproof heavy-duty roasting tin and quickly brown the lamb on all sides over a medium to high heat. Leave to cool completely.

Preheat the oven to 200C/400F/Gas 6. Stretch a good length of kitchen string on the work surface and overlap the branches of rosemary along the length of the string. Smear the sealed lamb joint all over with the black olive paste and place it on top of the rosemary at one end. Roll it up so it's completely encased and tie the string tightly to secure. It doesn't matter how crudely you do this as long as the rosemary stays in place.

Return the lamb to the roasting tin and drizzle with the remaining oil and the lemon juice. Roast for 15 minutes per 500g (1lb 2oz) plus an extra 15 minutes, turning the joint occasionally to ensure that it cooks evenly and the rosemary doesn't burn. Remove the cooked wrapped leg of lamb and leave to rest in a warm place for one-third of the time it took to cook.

Cut and remove the string. Carve the rested leg of lamb into slices and arrange on warmed plates to serve.

LAMB AND PRUNE TAGINE WITH COUSCOUS

The flavour of this tagine only improves with time: just leave it to cool and it will sit happily covered in the fridge for up to 2 days. This also gives the excess fat a chance to rise to the top so that it can be easily removed. I generally don't bother boning the shoulder of lamb myself as it can take a bit of time. It's much better to get your butcher to do it for you!

1 tbsp olive oil

1 onion, finely chopped

4 sweet potatoes, peeled and diced

2 garlic cloves, crushed

1kg (2lb 4oz) lamb shoulder, trimmed and cut into 1cm (1/2 inch) dice

400g can chopped tomatoes

100g (3 1/2 oz) dried prunes, stones removed and cut in half

salt and freshly ground black pepper

FOR THE COUSCOUS

375g (13oz) couscous

500ml (18fl oz) chicken stock

2 tbsp olive oil

1 tbsp toasted flaked almonds

100g (3 1/2 oz) dried prunes, stones removed and cut in half

. . . .

Serves 4

Heat a heavy-based pan over a medium heat. Add the olive oil and then the onion, sweet potatoes and garlic. Cover and leave to cook for 5 minutes, stirring once or twice. Add the lamb pieces and cook until well sealed and golden brown.

Stir the tomatoes and half the prunes into the lamb mixture and season to taste. Cover and leave to simmer for 2 hours or until the lamb is completely tender but still holding its shape, stirring occasionally to prevent the bottom from sticking.

To make the couscous, place the couscous in a large bowl. Bring the chicken stock to the boil in a pan and then pour over the couscous. Cover with a plate to act as a lid. Leave to soak for 10 minutes until all the liquid has been absorbed. Stir in the olive oil and separate the grains with a fork. Fold in the almonds and prunes.

Arrange a bed of couscous on warmed plates. Spoon over the lamb tagine and serve at once.

LAMB CHOPS WITH A HERB CRUST

Chump or loin chops are ideal for this recipe as are boneless leg chops. All are quick to cook and make a perfect main course for an impromptu dinner party. In Italy, they are traditionally served with a lemon wedge and some fried courgettes or potatoes.

Preheat the oven to 200C/400F/Gas 6. Heat a tablespoon of olive oil in an ovenproof frying pan large enough to take all of the lamb chops together. Cook the chops for 1–2 minutes on each side until golden brown.

Meanwhile, place the breadcrumbs in a bowl with the thyme and rosemary and season to taste. Drizzle over two tablespoons of the olive oil and stir until well combined.

Spread half of the mustard over the chops and then sprinkle over the breadcrumb topping, pressing down to ensure it sticks. Place in the oven for 10 minutes or until the breadcrumbs are crisp and lightly golden and the lamb is tender.

Heat the remaining olive oil in a frying pan. Tip in the leeks and sauté for 1 minute, then add the garlic and continue to cook for a minute or two. Fold in the butter with the rest of the mustard, the soured cream and parsley. Season to taste and allow to warm through.

Spoon the leek mixture onto warmed plates and arrange the lamb chops on top. Drizzle a little more olive oil over each one to serve.

4 tbsp olive oil, plus extra for drizzling
8 lamb chops
225g (8oz) leeks, trimmed and finely shredded
2 garlic cloves, crushed
55g (2oz) butter, diced
4 tbsp soured cream
2 tbsp chopped fresh flat-leaf parsley
salt and freshly ground black pepper

FOR THE HERB CRUST
200g (7oz) fresh white breadcrumbs
1 fresh thyme sprig, leaves stripped and finely chopped
1 fresh rosemary sprig, leaves stripped and finely chopped
4 tbsp Dijon mustard

. . . .

Serves 4

FINGER LICKIN' LAMB CHOPS WITH TOMATO SALAD

A perfect example of the motto 'the simpler the better'. If you're lucky enough to get your hands on some good, native new season's lamb, then this recipe is all you need for a truly tasty dish. If you have the time, leave to marinate for a couple of hours for maximum flavour.

8 leg of lamb chops
about 2 tbsp olive oil
1 ciabatta loaf, sliced on the diagonal
salt and freshly ground black pepper

FOR THE MARINADE
1 tsp coriander seeds
1 tsp cumin seeds
2 tbsp dark soy sauce
1 tbsp clear honey
1 tbsp tomato purée

FOR THE TOMATO SALAD
8 ripe plum tomatoes, seeded and diced
1 red onion, finely sliced
good handful mixed fresh herbs, such as
    flat-leaf parsley, mint and coriander
juice of 1 lemon
4 tbsp extra virgin olive oil

. . . .

Serves 4

To make the marinade, heat a small frying pan and toast the coriander and cumin seeds for 1 minute or until fragrant. Leave to cool and then transfer to a pestle and mortar. Grind to a fine powder. Place in a small pan with the soy sauce, honey and tomato purée. Stir to combine, then gently heat through.

Preheat a griddle pan until smoking hot. Remove the fat and any small bones from the lamb chops and then bash out with a meat mallet until about 1cm (½ inch) thick. Brush all over with the marinade. Brush a light coating of olive oil onto the griddle pan and then arrange the lamb chops on top (you may have to do this in batches depending on the size of your pan). Cook for 1 minute on a high heat on each side if you like your lamb rare; longer if you prefer it more well done. Transfer to warm plates and leave to rest for a couple of minutes.

Wipe the griddle pan and then use to toast the ciabatta bread slices for a minute or so on each side until lightly charred.

To make the tomato salad, place the tomatoes in a bowl with the red onion and herbs. Squeeze over the lemon juice and drizzle over the olive oil. Season to taste and stir to combine.

Arrange the slices of ciabatta in the centre of the plates. Top with the lamb chops and finish by spooning over the tomato salad to serve.

LAMB CUTLETS WITH PEA AND CHICKPEA MASH AND LEMON AND MINT PESTO

The wonderful flavours of spices in North African cookery hold a strong fascination for me. I love the combination of the spice and sweetness of the vegetables without the heat of chillies. The clean taste of the mint pesto is an excellent accompaniment for the lamb and you'll find yourself making it again and again.

To make the pesto, preheat the oven to 180C/350F/Gas 4. Spread the almonds on a baking sheet and toast in the oven until they are golden. Leave them to cool, and then tip them into a blender or small food processor. Add the mint, parsley, lemon rind, olive oil and Parmesan. Blitz until you have a rough paste and season to taste.

Place the lamb chops in a shallow dish and rub all over with the paprika and olive oil and season to taste. Heat a griddle or frying pan until very hot and cook the lamb for 6 minutes, turning halfway through, or longer if you prefer it more well-done. Briefly griddle the cherry tomatoes until the skins are about to burst. Once the lamb is cooked to your liking, leave it to rest for a few minutes.

To make the mash, bring the stock to the boil in a pan. Add the peas and boil for 2 minutes. Stir in the chickpeas and cook until they are heated through. Remove from the heat, add the lemon juice and season to taste. Roughly mash with a potato masher.

Divide the mash between warmed plates and add the rested lamb chops, griddled cherry tomatoes and a good spoonful of the pesto to serve.

12 small lamb cutlets, French trimmed
1 tsp paprika
1 tbsp olive oil
16 cherry tomatoes on the vine, cut into 4 individual branches
salt and freshly ground black pepper

FOR THE MASH
250ml (9fl oz) chicken stock
250g (9oz) frozen peas
400g can chickpeas, drained and rinsed
squeeze of lemon juice

FOR THE PESTO
55g (2oz) almonds, flaked or chopped
25g (1oz) fresh mint leaves
10g (1/4 oz) fresh flat-leaf parsley leaves
finely grated rind of 1 lemon
125ml (4fl oz) extra virgin olive oil
15g (1/2 oz) freshly grated Parmesan cheese

. . . .

Serves 4

LAMB BURGERS WITH SPICED TOMATO RELISH

This burger with a difference is always a winner. Grill, pan-fry or barbecue it to your liking. The burgers can be prepared in advance and the spiced tomato relish can be kept covered in the fridge for a couple of days, leaving very little to do at the last minute.

To make the burgers, place the lamb in a bowl with the red pepper, onion, chilli powder, tomato ketchup and basil. Season to taste and mix thoroughly until well combined. Divide the mixture into four portions and shape into 2.5cm (1 inch) thick burgers. Cover with cling film and chill until ready to cook.

To make the spiced tomato relish, heat the olive oil in a small pan. Add the onion, tomato, red pepper, sugar, chilli powder and red wine vinegar and season to taste. Bring to a simmer and cook for about 5 minutes until thickened. Remove from the heat and leave to cool, then stir in the parsley.

Heat a large frying pan. Add the olive oil and then add the burgers. Cook for 4 minutes on each side for rare; 6 minutes each side for medium-rare; 8–9 minutes each side for well-done. Season with salt.

Arrange the griddled bread on warmed plates and place a lamb burger on each one. Spoon the spiced tomato relish over the top to serve.

500g (1lb 2oz) minced lamb
½ red pepper, cored, seeded and finely chopped
½ onion, finely chopped
½ tsp chilli powder
1 tbsp tomato ketchup
handful fresh basil leaves, finely chopped
1 tbsp olive oil
salt and freshly ground black pepper
griddled bread, to serve

FOR THE RELISH
1 tbsp olive oil
½ onion, finely chopped
1 ripe tomato, seeded and diced
½ red pepper, seeded and finely chopped
½ tsp sugar
½ tsp chilli powder
1 tbsp red wine vinegar
handful fresh flat-leaf parsley leaves, finely chopped

. . . .

Serves 4

LAMB BOBOTIE

This is a South African dish made with spiced, minced meat baked with a custard topping. The recipe probably originates from the Dutch East India Company colonies in Batavia, with the name derived from the Indonesian Bobotok. Today there are different versions of the recipe all over Africa and as far reaching as Argentina, where the bobotie mixture is packed inside a large pumpkin and then baked until tender.

1 thick slice of bread
300ml (½ pint) milk
1 tbsp sunflower oil, plus extra
    for greasing
450g (1lb) minced lamb
25g (1oz) butter
1 small dessert apple, chopped
1 onion, finely chopped
½ tbsp curry powder
1 tbsp mango chutney
1 tbsp flaked almonds
1 tsp raisins
1 tbsp fresh lemon juice
2 eggs
salt and freshly ground black pepper
chopped fresh coriander, to garnish
boiled rice, to serve

. . . .

Serves 4

Preheat the oven to 180C/350F/Gas 4 and lightly grease a pie dish. Soak the bread in the milk for at least 10 minutes.

Heat the sunflower oil in a frying pan and then tip in the minced lamb and cook on a high heat for a few minutes until browned, breaking up any lumps with a wooden spoon.

Melt the butter in a separate frying pan and add the apple and onion. Cook slowly for about 5 minutes until the apple is soft and the onion is transparent. Stir in the curry powder and cook for another minute. Add the mango chutney, almonds, raisins and lemon juice.

Squeeze the milk from the bread, reserving the milk, and fork the bread into the meat mixture. Stir in the apple and onion mixture and season to taste. Spread the mixture into the pie dish and bake in the oven for 20 minutes until the meat has formed a light crust or skin.

Meanwhile, mix together the eggs and the reserved milk which the bread was soaked in, and season to taste. Remove the meat mixture from the oven and pour over the savoury custard. Return to the oven for 30–35 minutes or until the top is slightly browned. Garnish with the coriander.

Serve the bobotie straight to the table so that everyone can help themselves. Have a separate bowl of rice to hand around too.

MIKE ROBINSON

LAMB FILLET WITH FLAGEOLET BEANS AND LEEK CHUTNEY

Look out for neck fillet that has been boned out. It is a nice lean piece of meat that I like cutting up for kebabs. However, it is also perfect for grilling or frying quickly.

Place the sage, thyme, garlic and olive oil in a pestle and mortar and pound to a thick paste. Smear this all over the lamb fillets and set aside.

To make the chutney, heat the olive oil in a frying pan. Add the leeks and cook for a few minutes until softened but not coloured. Sprinkle over 100ml (3½ fl oz) of the balsamic vinegar with the sugar and cook for another 5 minutes on a medium-low heat until caramelized, stirring occasionally.

To make the flageolet beans, tip the beans into a pan with the red onion, garlic, thyme, tomatoes, parsley and olive oil. Place over a medium heat and simmer, stirring occasionally, for 3–4 minutes or until heated through. Stir in the balsamic vinegar and lemon juice and season to taste. Keep warm.

To cook the lamb, heat a heavy-based frying pan over a medium-high heat until hot. Add the lamb and sear for 2 minutes on each side, longer if you prefer your meat more well-done. Transfer to a warm plate.

Reduce the heat to medium-low and add a large glug of balsamic vinegar. Allow to sizzle for a few seconds, scraping any sediment from the bottom of the pan with a wooden spoon. Season to taste and stir into the leek chutney.

Spoon the flageolet beans onto warmed plates and arrange the lamb on top. Serve with the leek chutney.

2 tbsp chopped fresh sage
2 tbsp chopped fresh thyme
4 garlic cloves
2 tbsp olive oil
4 x 175g (6oz) lamb fillets, well trimmed
salt and freshly ground black pepper

FOR THE CHUTNEY
2 tbsp olive oil
2 leeks, finely shredded
about 125ml (4fl oz) balsamic vinegar
2 tsp light muscovado sugar

FOR THE BEANS
2 x 400g cans flageolet beans,
    drained and rinsed
1 large red onion, finely chopped
4 garlic cloves, finely chopped
4 fresh thyme sprigs
250g (9oz) cherry tomatoes, quartered
2 tbsp chopped fresh flat-leaf parsley
1 tbsp olive oil
good splash balsamic vinegar
juice of ½ lemon

Serves 4

poultry

SAFFRON AND GARLIC ONE-POT CHICKEN

Garlic mayonnaise is a wonderful way to thicken up a sauce without having to use any flour. This is a variation on one of the first dishes I ever cooked at home with any degree of success. Nostalgia aside, it's a tasty staple that freezes well. The better the saffron the better the dish, so either go to a reputable spice shop or try and bring some back from your holidays.

To make the garlic mayonnaise, place the mayonnaise in a small bowl and stir in the garlic. Set aside.

Heat the oil in a large heavy-based pan with a lid. Add the chicken pieces and cook until golden brown all over – you may have to do this in batches, depending on the size of your pan.

Add the red pepper to the browned chicken pieces with the chilli and lemon rind and cook for 2–3 minutes, stirring carefully. Pour in the stock and then tip in the potatoes, cumin and saffron with their water. Bring up to the boil, then cover and cook for 30–40 minutes or until the chicken and potatoes are cooked through and tender. The juices should run clear when the meat is pierced with a fine skewer.

Transfer the cooked chicken pieces and potatoes to a warmed serving bowl and keep warm. Add the leeks to the simmering stock and continue to cook until the stock has reduced by one third. Using a hand-held blender, blitz to a purée. Slowly beat in the garlic mayonnaise until thickened and then season to taste.

Pour the sauce over the chicken and potatoes and garnish with the parsley. Place directly on the table and have a basket of crusty bread to hand around separately.

1 tbsp olive oil
1 x 1.3 kg (3lb) roasting chicken, jointed
1 red pepper, cored, seeded and chopped
1/2 red chilli, seeded and finely chopped
finely grated rind of 1/2 lemon
1 pint (568ml) chicken stock
12 small new potatoes, scrubbed
pinch ground cumin
1 tsp saffron strands, soaked in a little warm water
2 leeks, trimmed and finely shredded
salt and freshly ground black pepper
chopped fresh flat-leaf parsley, to garnish
crusty bread, to serve

FOR THE GARLIC MAYONNAISE
2 tbsp mayonnaise
6 garlic cloves, crushed

. . . .

Serves 4

LEMON ROASTED CHICKEN WITH SHALLOT, ONION AND POTATO MASH

There is nothing more satisfying than sitting down to a complete roast chicken dinner. It's crucial to start off with the best chicken you can afford as you do get what you pay for. Excellent organic chicken is now more readily available and it's really worth it.

1 onion, cut into quarters and layers separated

1 garlic bulb, broken into cloves and peeled

1 bay leaf

1 fresh thyme sprig

juice of 1 lemon

4 tbsp olive oil

1.8kg (4lb) whole chicken, preferably free-range or organic

2 lemons

2 tbsp caster sugar

125ml (4fl oz) white wine

salt and freshly ground black pepper

steamed green beans, to serve

FOR THE MASH

8 shallots, halved

1 onion, halved

1/2 bulb garlic

2 tbsp olive oil

1 fresh thyme sprig

1 bay leaf

12 baby new potatoes

....

Serves 4

Preheat the oven to 220C/425F/Gas 7. Mix the onion in a bowl with the garlic, herbs, lemon juice, one tablespoon of the olive oil and the seasoning. Season the cavity of the chicken. Carefully ease the skin away from the breasts and stuff some of the mixture under the skin. Stuff the remainder into the cavity. Roll one of the lemons along on the work surface to soften and prick all over with a fork. Push into the cavity as well.

Make a slit down to the bone on each of the legs and tie them together with kitchen string. Place the chicken in a roasting tin. Season the outside of the bird generously and brush with half of the remaining olive oil. Slice the remaining lemon and arrange the slices on top, then sprinkle over the sugar. Roast for about 1 hour and 40 minutes or until the chicken is cooked through and the juices run clear when pierced.

For the mash, mix the shallots, onion, garlic, olive oil, thyme and bay leaf in a roasting tin. Roast for 30 minutes until softened.

Remove the cooked chicken from the oven and transfer to a platter. Leave to rest in a warm place for 15 minutes. Drain any excess fat and juices from the tin and reserve. Place the roasting tin directly on the hob and pour in the white wine. Reduce by two-thirds, scraping with a wooden spoon to release the sediment. Add a splash of water and reduce again until a couple of tablespoons are left. Whisk in the rest of the olive oil and pass through a sieve. Add the chicken juices and keep warm.

To make the mash, cook the potatoes in a pan of boiling salted water for 15–20 minutes until tender. Drain well, transfer to a bowl and lightly mash. Remove the skins from the cooked shallots, onion and garlic and mash roughly. Fold into the mashed potatoes. Add some of the reduced chicken juices to loosen.

Cut the string from the chicken and carve into slices. Serve with the mash and some steamed green beans, drizzled with the remaining chicken juices.

POACHED CHICKEN WITH FRESH HERBS AND SAUTEED WILD MUSHROOMS

This chicken is poached in a light, aromatic stock, that makes it very succulent. I've served it garnished with some delicious wild mushrooms and a drizzle of truffle oil, which compliment the flavour of the chicken perfectly.

Place all of the chicken pieces in a pan together with the onion, garlic and thyme and cover with 1.2 litres (2 pints) of water. Crumble in the chicken stock cube, season to taste and stir well to combine. Cover with a tight-fitting lid

Bring the chicken mixture to a gentle simmer and cook for 30 minutes or until the chicken pieces are cooked through and the juices run clear when pierced. Pick out the chicken, remove and discard the skin and set to one side. Strain the liquid into a clean pan and add the cream, then simmer for a few minutes until heated through. Put the chicken back in and stir through the tarragon and chervil.

Meanwhile, heat a large frying pan and add the butter. Tip in the mushrooms and fry for a few minutes, tossing occasionally, until golden and cooked through.

To make the croûtes, heat a griddle pan until hot. Brush the slices of baguette with olive oil on both sides. Place the bread on the griddle and lightly char on both sides.

Divide the poached chicken among warmed wide-rimmed bowls. Pour over some sauce and scatter the sautéed mushrooms on top. Finish with a drizzle of truffle oil and a toasted croûte. Serve the remaining croûtes on a separate plate with another dish of the steamed green beans so that everyone can help themselves

1.8kg (4lb) chicken, preferably free-range, jointed

1 onion, peeled

1/2 garlic bulb

1 fresh thyme sprig

1 chicken stock cube

300ml (1/2 pint) double cream

bunch fresh tarragon, leaves stripped and roughly chopped

bunch fresh chervil, leaves stripped and roughly chopped

25g (1oz) butter

10 shitake mushrooms, sliced

10 oyster mushrooms, sliced

1 baguette, cut into thick slices on a long angle

olive oil, for brushing

dash truffle oil

salt and freshly ground black pepper

steamed green beans, to serve

. . . .

Serves 4

INDONESIAN SPICY CHICKEN WITH SPICY GRAPEFRUIT SALAD

Chicken thighs are not only cheaper than breasts but they are also much tastier. Their secret is being able to withstand long cooking that would leave a breast fillet dry and tasteless. When cooking thighs this way, you end up with a succulent, well-flavoured dish.

2lb (900g) skinless chicken thighs
with the bone in

FOR THE MARINADE

6 tbsp finely chopped shallots

3 tbsp coarsely chopped garlic

3 tbsp finely chopped lime or lemon rind

3 fresh red or green chillies, seeded
and chopped

4 kaffir lime leaves, crushed

2 tsp finely chopped fresh root ginger

1 tsp ground turmeric

2 tsp ground coriander

1 tsp salt

1 tsp freshly ground black pepper

5 tbsp coconut milk (from a carton or can)

FOR THE SALAD

2 large grapefruits or 1 large pomelo

2 tbsp vegetable oil

3 tbsp finely diced shallots

3 tbsp finely sliced garlic

2 small Thai red chillies, seeded and
finely chopped

3 tbsp roasted chopped peanuts

3 tbsp finely shredded spring onions

2 tbsp dried chopped shrimps

2 tbsp fresh lime juice

1 tbsp Thai fish sauce (nam pla)

1 tbsp sugar

handful fresh coriander leaves, to garnish

. . . .

Serves 4

To prepare the marinade, place the shallots in a blender or pestle and mortar with the garlic, lime or lemon rind, chillies, lime leaves, ginger, turmeric, coriander, salt, pepper and coconut milk. Blend to a purée and then transfer to a bowl.

Blot the chicken thighs dry with kitchen paper and add to the marinade, stirring until well combined. Cover with cling film and chill over night. Remove the chicken from the fridge and leave at room temperature for 40 minutes before cooking.

Make a charcoal fire in the barbecue or preheat the oven grill to high. When the charcoal is ash white or the oven grill is very hot, grill the chicken for 10 minutes on each side or until cooked all the way through and the juices run clear when pierced.

To make the grapefruit salad, peel the grapefruits or pomelo and separate the segments, removing any skin or membrane. Gently break the flesh into pieces and place in a large bowl.

Heat a wok until hot, add the oil and stir-fry the shallots and garlic until they are golden brown. Remove and drain on kitchen paper.

Add the browned shallots and garlic to the bowl of grapefruit. Add the chillies, peanuts, spring onions and shrimps and gently mix well.

Combine the lime juice, fish sauce and sugar. Pour over the grapefruit mixture and toss carefully together. Arrange on a platter and garnish with the coriander leaves.

Place the cooked Indonesian chicken on a warmed platter and serve immediately or allow to cool and serve at room temperature with the grapefruit salad.

SOUTHERN FRIED CHICKEN WITH BOURBON GRAVY

This fried chicken is the best you'll have ever tasted – deep-fried moist, juicy meat encased in a shatteringly crisp coating. The origins of this dish come from the Deep South where it continues to be served as the national dish on Independence Day and special holidays.

4 chicken thighs
4 chicken drumsticks
400ml (14fl oz) vegetable oil
50ml (2fl oz) bourbon
1 onion, finely sliced
200ml (7fl oz) chicken stock
mashed potato, to serve

FOR THE MARINADE
finely grated rind and juice of 1 lemon
2 tsp Cajun seasoning
1 tsp salt
1 tsp ground black pepper
1 tbsp olive oil

FOR THE COATING
150g (5½ oz) plain flour
1 tbsp Cajun seasoning
1 tsp salt
1 tsp ground black pepper
1 tsp garlic powder

. . . .

Serves 4

To make the marinade, place the lemon rind and juice in a shallow non-metallic dish with the Cajun seasoning, salt, pepper and olive oil. Mix well and then add the chicken, turning to coat evenly. Cover with cling film and chill overnight in the fridge to allow the flavours to penetrate.

To make the coating, mix together the plain flour in a shallow bowl with the Cajun seasoning, salt, pepper and garlic powder. When you are ready to cook the chicken, heat the vegetable oil in a large frying pan with a lid.

Remove the chicken from the marinade, shaking off any excess. Toss the chicken pieces in the seasoned flour until fully coated. Reserve a tablespoon of the seasoned flour to use in the gravy. Add the chicken to the frying pan, skin-side down. Cook for a few minutes until golden brown, then turn over and cover the pan. Cook for a further 6–10 minutes, then uncover and turn again. Continue to cook for another 5 minutes or until the chicken is cooked through and the juices run clear when pierced.

To make the gravy, drain off the oil from the pan but leave the brown crust in the bottom. Add the bourbon and use to deglaze, scraping the bottom with a wooden spoon. Add the onion and cook for a few minutes until slightly softened.

Mix a tablespoon of the remaining coating mixture with a little water to make a paste. Add to the softened onion and allow to cook for 1 minute, stirring. Gradually add the stock, stirring after each addition until smooth, and cook for about 5 minutes until reduced and thickened.

Put a heaped pile of mash on each warmed plate and make a well in the centre. Pour the gravy into the well and top with the crunchy southern fried chicken.

HONEY AND CORIANDER GLAZED CHICKEN WITH SHOPSKA SALAD

I went to Bulgaria on holiday recently and ate a version of this at a local restaurant two or three times. The salad is named after the Shoppi, or natives of Sofia. It's perfect in the summertime, when tomatoes are at their most flavoursome.

Preheat the oven to 200C/400F/Gas 6 and heat a heavy-based frying pan until very hot. To make the glaze for the chicken, mix together the honey, coriander, fennel and ginger in a small bowl.

Season the chicken and place skin-side down in the heated frying pan. Cook for about 2–3 minutes until browned. Turn over and brush with the glaze. Transfer to the oven and cook for a further 20–30 minutes or until the chicken is cooked through and tender and the juices run clear when pierced.

Meanwhile, make the Shopska salad. Mix together the cucumber, spring onions, pepper and tomatoes in a large bowl. Pile up the mixture in a salad dish. Drizzle with the olive oil and vinegar. Grate over the feta cheese to form a "snow cap", then scatter over the olives and parsley.

Arrange the chicken on warmed plates and serve with the bowl of Shopska salad.

80ml (3fl oz) clear honey
4 tsp coriander seeds, coarsely ground
4 tsp fennel seeds
2 tbsp freshly grated root ginger
4 chicken thighs
4 chicken legs
salt and freshly ground black pepper

FOR THE SHOPSKA SALAD
1 cucumber, cut into cubes
6 spring onions, roughly chopped
1 green pepper, cut into cubes
3 large tomatoes, cut into cubes
3 tbsp olive oil
3 tbsp white wine vinegar
150g (5 1/2 oz) feta cheese
10 black olives
small bunch flat-leaf parsley, leaves stripped and finely chopped

Serves 4

CHICKEN ENCHILADAS WITH PICKLED CUCUMBER

Recently I was lucky enough to travel to Mexico, where I tasted some incredible dishes. Enchiladas are most commonly made with corn tortillas although in northern Mexico where I had them soft flour tortillas are also sometimes used.

3 tbsp olive oil

2 large onions, finely sliced

2 courgettes, cut into fine strips

600g (1lb 5oz) skinless and boneless chicken breast fillets, cut in strips

1 tsp dried oregano

1 tsp ground cumin

1 tsp caster sugar

3 tbsp tomato purée

125ml (4fl oz) chicken stock

2 tbsp chopped fresh flat-leaf parsley

8 soft flour tortillas

300g (10½ oz) Cheddar, grated

salt and freshly ground black pepper

FOR THE PICKLED CUCUMBER

2 cucumbers, halved, seeded and cut into fine strips

1 medium hot red chilli, seeded and finely sliced

juice of 2 limes

2 tbsp chopped fresh coriander

5 tbsp white wine vinegar

1 tsp caster sugar

3 tbsp extra virgin olive oil

. . . .

Serves 4

Preheat the oven to 180C/350F/Gas 4. Heat a large pan with the olive oil and fry the onions and courgettes for a few minutes until softened but not coloured. Add the chicken and continue to fry for about 2 minutes until the meat starts to change colour.

Add the oregano to the pan with the cumin, sugar and tomato purée and season to taste, stirring well to combine. Cook for a further minute and then add in the chicken stock. Allow to cook for another 3 minutes until the sauce thickens then stir in the parsley.

Meanwhile, warm the tortillas on a dry frying pan for 20 seconds on each side. Keep the tortillas soft and warm by placing them into a folded, slightly damp tea towel, then fill with the chicken mixture and roll them like a big cigar. Place them in an ovenproof dish and cover with the grated Cheddar. Place in the oven for 15 minutes or until the cheese is golden and bubbling and the chicken is cooked through.

To make the pickled cucumber, place the cucumber in a bowl and add the chilli, lime juice, coriander, vinegar, sugar and extra virgin olive oil. Season to taste and leave to marinate for 20 minutes.

Serve the enchiladas with the bowl of pickled cucumber.

SPICY FRIED CHICKEN WITH APPLE SALAD

This fragrant chicken eats very well with the simple apple salad. The yoghurt marinade coagulates around the meat, giving you a dish that is stunning in flavour, texture and colour. Of course one of the beauties of it is just how easy it is to make.

4 large skinless and boneless chicken breast fillets, cut into thin strips or pieces
1–2 tbsp sunflower oil
squeeze of lemon juice
1–2 tbsp chopped fresh coriander
salt and freshly ground black pepper

FOR THE MARINADE
4 tbsp natural yoghurt
juice of 2 limes
1 tsp ground turmeric
1 tsp paprika
good pinch ground cardamom
2 garlic cloves, crushed
pinch of salt

FOR THE SALAD
50g (2oz) rocket
85g (3oz) watercress
1 green apple, cored and sliced
1 red apple, cored and sliced
3 shallots, sliced into rings
handful of sultanas and raisins
6 tbsp olive oil
1 tbsp balsamic vinegar
1 tbsp sherry vinegar
squeeze of lemon juice

To make the marinade, mix together the yoghurt in a bowl with the lime juice, turmeric, paprika, cardamom, garlic and pinch of salt. Add the chicken strips and stir so that they become totally covered.

Heat a wok or frying pan with 1 tablespoon of the oil. When the pan is very hot, add the chicken pieces and stir fry for 5–6 minutes or until the chicken is cooked through and tender and the juices run clear when pierced. Add a little more oil if you find the mixture sticking to the bottom of the wok.

To make the salad, mix the rocket, watercress, apples, shallots, sultanas and raisins together in a large bowl. Quickly mix up the dressing by placing the olive oil in a small bowl with the vinegars and lemon juice and season to taste.

When ready to serve, add the dressing to the apple salad and toss well to combine. Pile the spicy chicken onto warmed plates and squeeze over the lemon juice. Sprinkle over the coriander and serve with the apple salad.

. . . .

Serves 4

BLACK PEPPER CHICKEN CURRY

This is my version of a dish that is originally from Southern India. It's a great combination, with the chicken picking up the flavours of all the spices. It goes beautifully with freshly baked naan bread. A dish fit for a king!

To make the marinade, mix the salt in a shallow non-metallic dish with the garlic, grated ginger, lemon juice, turmeric, yoghurt and pepper. Stir in the chicken and leave, covered with clingfilm, to marinate for 30 minutes.

Heat the oil in a pan and stir in the black pepper and finely chopped ginger. Add the onions and cook for 6–8 minutes or until they caramelize to a golden brown colour.

Add the chicken with the marinade to the pan and cook for another 7–10 minutes or until the moisture dries up. Pour in 100ml (3½ fl oz) of water and simmer until the chicken is cooked through and tender and the juices run clear when pierced. Fold in the finely sliced ginger, and chopped coriander leaves and transfer to a warmed dish.

Garnish the black pepper curry with a little more black pepper and the mustard cress and serve with plenty of warmed naan bread to mop up all those delicious juices.

4 skinless and boneless chicken
  breast fillets, cut into strips
3 tbsp vegetable oil
1 tsp freshly ground black pepper
1 tbsp finely chopped root ginger
4 onions, finely sliced
1 tbsp finely sliced root ginger
2 tbsp chopped fresh coriander
freshly ground black pepper and
  mustard cress, to garnish
warmed naan breads, to serve

FOR THE MARINADE
½ tsp salt
1 tsp crushed garlic
1 tsp finely grated root ginger
2 tbsp fresh lemon juice
1 tsp ground turmeric
3 tbsp natural yoghurt
1 tsp freshly ground black pepper

. . . .

Serves 4

DUCK BREAST WITH SAGE AND BLACK PEPPER AND CARROT AND PARSNIP MASH

This is a delicious way of jazzing up duck breasts. For a professional finish score the skin into a diamond pattern with the tip of a sharp knife, taking care that you don't cut through to the meat. They are best served slightly pink in the centre, but just cook them for a bit longer if you prefer them well done.

4 x 200g (7oz) duck breasts
2 tbsp olive oil
55g (2oz) butter
200ml (7fl oz) fresh beef stock
6 fresh sage leaves
50ml (2fl oz) balsamic vinegar
½ tsp honey
½ tsp crushed black peppercorns
salt and freshly ground black pepper

FOR THE MASH
6 carrots, sliced
6 parsnips, sliced
3–4 tbsp softened butter

FOR THE BUTTERED CABBAGE
½ cabbage, tough core removed
  and shredded
25g (1oz) butter

. . . .

Serves 4

Preheat the oven to 180C/350F/Gas 4. Trim the excess fat and sinew from the duck breasts and season on both sides. Heat an ovenproof frying pan until very hot and add the olive oil. Add a little of the butter and once foaming add the breasts, skin-side down. Cook for 3 minutes or until the skin is golden and crisp.

Pour the beef stock into a small pan and reduce by half. Meanwhile, turn the breasts over and add in four of the sage leaves and cook for a further 2 minutes. Remove the sage leaves from the pan and set to one side. Transfer the duck to the oven and cook for a further 7 minutes or until cooked to your liking. Remove from the oven and leave to rest. Pour off any excess fat from the pan and reserve to use in the buttered cabbage.

Deglaze the pan with the balsamic vinegar then add the reduced stock, honey and crushed peppercorns. Bring to a simmer then whisk in the rest of the butter. Shred the remaining two sage leaves and stir into the sauce. Season to taste.

To make the carrot and parsnip mash, bring a pan of salted water to the boil and add the carrots. Cook for 5 minutes then add the parsnips and continue to cook until both are tender but not too soft. Drain well, then mash with the butter. Season to taste and keep warm.

To make the buttered cabbage, blanch the cabbage in a pan of boiling water for 20 seconds or so, then drain and quickly refresh under cold running water. Heat a frying pan until hot then add the reserved duck fat and the butter. Tip in the cabbage and stir fry for a minute or so until slightly softened. Season to taste.

Slice each duck breast into four. Divide the cabbage and mash between warmed plates, fan out the duck pieces on top and drizzle over the sauce. Garnish with the fried sage.

THAI DUCK CURRY

You'll only need three tablespoons of the curry paste for this dish but the remainder can be kept in a small, lidded jar in the fridge for up to four weeks. Simply cover with a thin layer of vegetable oil to help keep it fresh. The hotness will vary according to the type of chillies used. You can always add a few seeds if you like it very hot.

2 x 175g (6oz) duck breasts, well trimmed
2 tbsp vegetable oil
700ml (1¼ pints) coconut milk
250ml (9fl oz) coconut cream
200g (7oz) frozen peas
200g (7oz) cherry tomatoes, halved
2 tbsp Thai fish sauce (nam pla)
1 tbsp Demerara sugar
4 kaffir lime leaves, torn
1 star anise
1 tbsp green peppercorns
2 fresh red chillies, sliced on the diagonal
handful fresh basil, roughly chopped
handful fresh coriander, roughly chopped
handful fresh mint, roughly chopped
steamed jasmine rice, to serve

FOR THE CURRY PASTE:
7 long dried red chillies, seeded
1 tsp cumin seeds
1½ tsp coriander seeds
5 whole cloves
¼ tsp freshly grated nutmeg
2 tbsp finely sliced lemon grass
2 tbsp finely sliced red shallots
1 tbsp finely chopped garlic
finely grated rind of 2 limes
10 white peppercorns
large pinch salt
½ tsp shrimp paste

Heat a dry frying pan until it is quite hot. Add the duck breasts skin-side down, lower the heat to medium and cook for 3–4 minutes until the skin is crisp and golden brown. Turn the breasts over and cook them for another 5 minutes, or a little longer if you don't like your duck too pink. Transfer to a plate and leave to cool, then trim away the fat and cut into slices. Set aside.

To make the curry paste, soak the chillies in a bowl of hot water for about 15 minutes, then drain well on kitchen paper. Heat a wok and dry roast the cumin and coriander seeds with the cloves for 40–50 seconds until they have released their aroma. Transfer to a mini blender or pestle and mortar and grind to a powder. Place the chillies in a food processor with the ground spices, nutmeg, lemon grass, shallots, garlic, lime rind, peppercorns, salt and shrimp paste and blitz to combine. Measure out 3 tablespoons – the remainder can be used another day.

Heat a large wok until very hot. Add the oil and swirl up the sides, then stir in the curry paste and cook for 2 minutes. Pour in the coconut milk and cream and bring to a gentle simmer. Add the reserved duck slices with the peas and cherry tomatoes. Cook for a couple of minutes until heated through, stirring occasionally. Season with the Thai fish sauce and sugar, stirring well to combine. Add in the lime leaves, star anise and green peppercorns and simmer for another minute.

Spoon into individual warmed bowls and scatter over the red chillies, basil, coriander and mint. Serve hot with bowls of steamed jasmine rice.

Serves 4

TURKEY STROGANOFF

One of those dishes that everyone still seems to enjoy – a classic 1970s dinner party delight! It's deeply unfashionable, but who cares? Whenever I eat it, I love it. Traditionally it was made with beef and served with a mixture of fluffy white and wild rice or buttered noodles.

Preheat the oven to 180C/350F/Gas 4. Place four of the mushrooms in a small baking tin and sprinkle over the garlic, parsley, thyme and butter, then season to taste. Bake for 10 minutes until just tender and cooked through. Chop up the remaining two mushrooms and set aside.

Heat half the olive oil in a pan and add the onion. Sweat gently for about 5 minutes, stirring occasionally, until softened.

Heat the rest of the olive oil in a frying pan. Place the flour in a shallow dish with the paprika and season to taste, then use to dust the turkey strips. Add the coated turkey strips to the heated frying pan and cook for 3–4 minutes or until lightly browned and cooked through.

Pour the white wine into the softened onions and allow to bubble down, then stir in the Dijon mustard, Worcestershire sauce, cream and reserved chopped mushrooms. Cook for 3 minutes or until the mushrooms are tender, stirring occasionally. Fold in the cooked turkey strips and allow to heat through.

Arrange some rice on each warmed plate with a baked mushroom. Spoon over the turkey stroganoff and garnish with a lemon wedge to serve.

6 large flat mushrooms
4 garlic cloves, finely chopped
2 tbsp chopped fresh flat-leaf parsley
1/2 tsp chopped fresh thyme
55g (2oz) butter, diced
4 tbsp olive oil
1 large onion, diced
2 tbsp plain flour
1 tsp paprika
4 turkey fillets, cut into strips
225ml (8fl oz) white wine
4 tbsp Dijon mustard
good dash Worcestershire sauce
125ml (4fl oz) double cream
salt and freshly ground black pepper
boiled white rice, to serve
lemon wedges, to garnish

. . . .

Serves 4

CRISPY SPICED POUSSIN WITH COCONUT SPINACH

Poussins are the smallest chickens that you can buy. I like them because they are so tender and quick to cook. I can get them in my local butchers already spatchcocked, which saves a bit of a job. Otherwise you can do it yourself with poultry shears or sharp kitchen scissors.

Place one tablespoon of the sunflower oil in a mini food processor or liquidizer with the ginger, chilli sauce, fish sauce, coriander and sesame oil. Blend to a smooth paste.

Slash the legs of the poussins with a sharp knife, then gently lift the skin away from the breasts and put a little of the paste underneath, rubbing it into the meat really well. Smother the remaining paste all over the poussins, put them in a dish and cover with clingfilm. Leave to marinate for a couple of hours or preferably overnight in the fridge.

When ready to cook, preheat the oven to 190C/375F/Gas 5. Heat two large ovenproof frying pans and add half of the remaining sunflower oil to each one. Add the poussins, skin-side down, and cook for 1–2 minutes, then turn over and place in the oven for a further 15–25 minutes (you can transfer them to a roasting tin if you prefer) or until cooked through and lightly charred and the juices run clear when pierced. The cooking time will depend on the size of the poussins.

Meanwhile, prepare the spinach. Place the garlic and sweet chilli sauce in a wok and heat through for 1 minute. Pour in the coconut cream and add the chilli. Bring to a simmer, then reduce the heat and cook gently for 3–4 minutes. Add the lime juice, fish sauce and spinach and cook for another few minutes until just wilted, tossing the wok occasionally.

Divide the spinach between warmed wide-rimmed bowls and top each one with a crispy spiced poussin.

4 tbsp sunflower oil
2 tsp freshly grated root ginger
4 tbsp sweet chilli sauce
good dash Thai fish sauce (nam pla)
large handful fresh coriander leaves
4 tsp toasted sesame oil
4 poussins, spatchcocked

FOR THE SPINACH
4 garlic cloves, finely chopped
2 tbsp sweet chilli sauce
500ml (18fl oz) coconut cream
2 red chillies, split and seeded
juice of 2 limes
2 tbsp Thai fish sauce (nam pla)
175g (6oz) spinach, (not baby), thick
   stalks removed

Serves 4

fish

EXCEEDINGLY GOOD DOUBLE FISH PIE

A good fish pie is perfect for the family and is an ideal dish to prepare ahead. Avoid smoked haddock that has been dyed with tartrazine – easy to spot as the fish will be golden yellow. Other white fish such as cod or hake can be used instead of the haddock – use what is fresh and available.

Butter a 2 litre (3½ pint) shallow pie dish, about 6cm (2½ inches) deep. Cut the fish into 1cm (½ inch) pieces, discarding any bones.

Place the eggs in a small pan and just cover with boiling water. Cook for about 10 minutes until hard-boiled. Drain, rinse under cold running water, then remove the shells and roughly chop.

Cook the leeks in a pan of boiling salted water for about 5 minutes and then drain well. Heat the milk in a separate small pan until hot.

Melt the butter in a good sized pan, add the flour and cook for a few moments, not allowing it to colour. Whisk in half the hot milk and allow to thicken. Whisk in the remaining hot milk and continue to whisk until smooth.

Add the fish pieces to the white sauce and season to taste. Cook for 2 minutes, stirring continuously. Stir in the lemon juice, dill and chopped hard-boiled eggs and pour into the buttered dish. Spoon over the leeks and set aside until the mixture has become completely cold and firm.

Preheat the oven to 180C/350F/Gas 4. Meanwhile, make the topping. Cook the potatoes in a pan of boiling salted water for 15–20 minutes until tender. Drain well and then push the potatoes to one side in the pan. Add the milk and let it become hot, then, using a potato masher, mash the potatoes with the milk. Beat in the mustard and season to taste.

Spread the mash over the cooled fish mixture and scatter the Cheddar on top. Stand the dish in a large roasting tin (just in case it boils over) and bake for about 30 minutes until the top is golden and the sauce is bubbling at the edges.

Serve the fish pie straight away with a bowl of mixed salad.

55g (2oz) butter, plus extra for greasing
350g (12oz) un-dyed smoked haddock fillet, skinned
350g (12oz) haddock fillet, skinned
3 eggs
2 leeks, trimmed and sliced
568ml (1 pint) milk
55g (2oz) butter
55g (2oz) plain flour
juice of ½ lemon
2 tbsp chopped fresh dill
salt and freshly ground black pepper
lightly dressed mixed salad, to serve

FOR THE TOPPING
1kg (2¼lb) potatoes, peeled and cut into even-sized pieces
300ml (½ pint) milk
2 heaped tbsp wholegrain mustard
85g (3oz) mature Cheddar, grated

. . . .

Serves 6–8

SMOKED HADDOCK BOUILLABAISSE

This wonderful substantial soup makes a meal in itself with the crusty pesto garlic bread. Of course it isn't a bouillabaisse in the strictest sense of the word. But it does have similarities to the world famous Provençal fish soup, hence the name.

55g (2oz) butter
1 leek, trimmed and thinly sliced
1 carrot, cut into 1cm (½ inch) cubes
250g (9oz) potatoes, cut into 1cm
    (½ inch) cubes
40g (1½ oz) plain flour
568ml (1 pint) fish or vegetable stock
568ml (1 pint) milk
500g (1lb 2oz) undyed smoked haddock,
    skinned and cut into bite-sized pieces
2 tbsp chopped fresh dill
salt and freshly ground black pepper

FOR THE PESTO GARLIC BREAD
55g (2oz) butter, softened
1 garlic clove, crushed
55g (2oz) freshly grated Parmesan
2 tbsp green pesto (homemade or
    shop-bought)
2 tbsp chopped fresh flat-leaf parsley
2 ready-to-bake baguettes

Serves 4–6

Preheat the oven to 200C/400F/Gas 6. Heat the butter in a large pan. Add the leek and carrot and fry over a high heat for a minute or two, stirring. Add the potatoes, tossing to combine, then sprinkle over the flour. Cook for a few minutes, stirring. Heat the stock in a separate pan until hot.

Gradually add the hot stock to the leek, carrot and potato mixture, stirring until smooth after each addition. Simmer for a few minutes to thicken. Season with pepper (no salt at this stage). Bring to the boil, cover and simmer for about 10 minutes until the vegetables are tender.

Meanwhile, make the pesto garlic bread. Place the butter in a small bowl with the garlic, Parmesan, pesto and parsley. Mix until well combined. Slice each baguette into six diagonal slices, spread half of the butter mixture between each slice and reassemble the baguettes on a foil-covered baking sheet. Spread the rest of the butter mixture over the top of the baguettes and bake for about 8–10 minutes until the baguettes are lightly browned and piping hot.

Pour the milk into the stock and cooked vegetable mixture, stirring until smooth, then add the smoked haddock and simmer gently for about 5 minutes until the fish is just cooked through and tender. Season to taste and stir in the dill.

Break up the pesto garlic bread into slices and pile into a bowl, then serve with the fish bouillabaisse.

HALIBUT CURRY WITH CHAPATIS

Traditionally, a curry of this type is made with pomfret, the white-fleshed non-oily fish found along the Mumbai coastline. The Dover sole's size and bone structure is the most similar, but if you're not feeling particularly flush, halibut gives an excellent result.

Mix together the turmeric, salt and chilli powder, then rub it all over the fish fillets, coating the flesh well. Set aside for 5 minutes.

Meanwhile, make the chapatis. Set aside 100g (3½oz) of the flour for shaping the chapatis. Place the rest of the flour in a deep bowl. Add 200ml (7fl oz) of water a little at a time, kneading as you go until you have a soft, elastic dough. The longer you knead the chapati dough the softer the bread will be.

Place the garlic, green chillies, cumin, ginger and coriander leaves in a food processor or liquidizer with 125ml (4fl oz) of water. Blend to a thick purée.

Heat the oil in a large frying pan. Add the spice-coated fish and cook for 2–3 minutes until lightly golden. Turn over and pour in the garlic purée, then simmer gently for about 3 minutes, until the fish is cooked through and tender.

To finish making the chapatis, sprinkle a little flour on to a flat surface or board. Divide the dough into eight and shape each piece into a ball. Flatten the balls slightly then place on the floured surface and roll out each one into a thin disc about 15cm (6 inches) in diameter.

Heat a griddle or shallow frying pan. Lay a disc onto the hot pan and leave for 20 to 30 seconds until the surface is bubbly. Flip over and cook the other side for 10 to 15 seconds. As soon as brown spots appear on the underside it's done. Place a sheet of kitchen paper between each disc to absorb the excess oil.

Mix the tamarind with 50ml (2fl oz) of water and stir into the fish curry, then cook for another minute until heated through.

Spoon the halibut curry onto warmed plates and serve with the chapatis on the side.

½ tsp ground turmeric
¼ tsp salt
¼ tsp chilli powder
4 x 300g (10½ oz) fresh halibut fillets, skinned
4 garlic cloves
2 green chillies, stalks removed
1 tsp ground cumin
2.5cm (1 inch) piece root ginger, peeled
handful fresh coriander leaves, roughly chopped
2 tbsp groundnut oil
1 tsp tamarind concentrate

FOR THE CHAPATIS
350g (12oz) wholemeal plain flour

. . . .

Serves 4

COD WITH BLOOD ORANGES AND CORIANDER

ANTONY WORRALL THOMPSON

Blood oranges are the predominant flavour in this delightful fish dish. They grow mostly in Mediterranean countries, especially Italy where the combination of cold winter nights and mild days favours the development of anthocyanins, the red pigments which give them their distinctive deep red colour. Look out for the round Moro variety or the Tarocco, which is supposed to be one of the world's finest tasting citrus fruits.

4 x 150g (5oz) cod fillets, boned
3 blood oranges
4 spring onions, cut into fine strips
good pinch ground coriander
4cm (1½ inch) root ginger, peeled and
   finely grated
2 tbsp sweet chilli sauce
2 tbsp chopped fresh coriander
salt and freshly ground black pepper

. . . .

Serves 4

Preheat the oven to 200C/400F/Gas 6 and heat a large frying pan. Season the cod fillets, then add to the pan and cook for 2 minutes on each side.

Transfer the sealed fish fillets to a shallow baking dish. Using a very sharp knife, remove the skin and white pith from two of the blood oranges, then cut into segments. Scatter over the fish with the spring onions.

Reheat the frying pan. Finely grate the rind from the remaining orange and then squeeze out the juice. Add to the pan with the ground coriander, ginger and sweet chilli sauce. Simmer gently for 2–3 minutes until the sauce is slightly reduced and thickened. Season to taste.

Pour the sauce over the fish, then cover with non-stick parchment paper or foil. Bake for 10–12 minutes until cooked through and tender.

Transfer the cod fillets to warmed plates and spoon over the sauce. Scatter over the fresh coriander and serve at once.

COD WITH PESTO CRUST AND AUBERGINE MASH

This Merluzzo al Pesto proves just how easy it is to bring a taste of Italy into your kitchen. It's a brilliant way to cook cod; my mum used to make a similar dish but she used salt cod, which she soaked overnight and then made into a version of this recipe.

extra virgin olive oil, for cooking

4 x 150g (5oz) cod fillets, scaled and boned

Maldon sea salt and ground black pepper

cooked baby spinach, to serve

FOR THE AUBERGINE MASH

225g (8oz) aubergine

2 tbsp olive oil, plus extra for drizzling

225g (8oz) potatoes, cut into quarters

50ml (2fl oz) double cream

pinch freshly grated nutmeg

1 tbsp roughly chopped fresh coriander

1 garlic clove, crushed

FOR THE PESTO CRUST

30 fresh basil leaves

55g (2oz) sun-dried tomatoes in olive oil, drained

3 garlic cloves, crushed

25g (1oz) pine nuts

25g (1oz) freshly grated Parmesan

25g (1oz) Pecorino cheese, grated

3 tbsp extra virgin olive oil

55g (2oz) butter, melted

55g (2oz) fresh wholemeal breadcrumbs

finely grated rind and juice of 1 lemon

. . . .

Serves 4

Preheat the oven to 180C/350F/Gas 4. Place the aubergine in a roasting tin, sprinkle with sea salt and drizzle over a little extra virgin olive oil. Roast for 25–30 minutes or until soft. Leave until cool enough to handle.

Meanwhile, cook the potatoes in a pan of boiling salted water for 15–20 minutes until tender, then drain well. Mash with the cream, nutmeg and half of the olive oil until smooth.

To make the pesto for the crust, place the basil leaves, sun-dried tomatoes, garlic, pine nuts, Parmesan and Pecorino in a food processor or liquidizer and blitz for 30 seconds. With the machine running, slowly add the olive oil until it's all combined. Season to taste.

Melt the butter in a small pan or in the microwave and stir in the breadcrumbs, lemon juice and rind. Allow to cool and then mix with three quarters of the pesto to make the crust. Reserve the remaining pesto.

Increase the oven temperature to 200C/400F/Gas 6. Place a teaspoon of extra virgin olive oil in a non-stick frying pan and heat until almost smoking. Place the fish skin-side down in the pan and cook for 1½ minutes, then turn over and cook for a further 1½ minutes. Place the fish skin-side down on an oiled baking sheet. Pat the pesto crust mix on top of the cod and bake in the oven for 8 minutes until cooked through and tender.

Scoop out the inside of the aubergine with a spoon and mash lightly or roughly blitz with a hand blender. Add the coriander, garlic and remaining olive oil and mix well to combine. Fold in the mashed potatoes and season to taste.

Place some spinach in the middle of each warmed plate and top with the aubergine mash followed by the pesto-crusted cod. Drizzle with the remaining pesto to serve.

SEABASS WITH LEEK CARBONARA

Sea bass is a superb fish to cook and eat. It can be quite expensive, but is certainly worth paying for. Other fish, such as cod, salmon or sole, can be used in its place. The fish is always best cooked at the last moment so you appreciate all its freshness. Once you start frying it may need to be gently pressed down with a fish slice to stop it curling up.

Dry the sea bass fillets on kitchen paper, then season to taste and lightly dust the skin with the flour.

Heat the olive oil in a large non-stick frying pan and add the butter. Once the butter begins to sizzle, add the fish, skin-side down. Leave to cook for 6–7 minutes or until the skin is crisp and coloured. Turn over and remove from the heat, the residual heat in the pan will continue to cook the fish.

To make the leek carbonara, heat a large pan with a lid and add the bacon. Fry for a few minutes, stirring occasionally, until it's golden and crisp. Transfer the bacon to a plate and pour away any excess fat from the pan.

Add the butter to the pan and once it has melted, stir in the leeks along with three tablespoons of water. Cover the leeks and leave to steam for a few minutes until tender. Pour in the cream and simmer, stirring continuously, until lightly thickened. Stir through the Parmesan and cooked bacon, then finish with the lemon juice. Season to taste.

Spoon the leek carbonara onto warmed plates and top with the sea bass fillets to serve.

4 x 175g (6oz) sea bass fillets, skin on
plain flour, for dusting
a little olive oil
large knob butter
salt and freshly ground black pepper

FOR THE LEEK CARBONARA
6 rindless streaky bacon rashers, cut into thin strips
large knob of butter
3 leeks, trimmed, halved and finely chopped
150ml (¼ pint) double cream
2 tbsp freshly grated Parmesan
squeeze of lemon

. . . .

Serves 4

HOT SMOKED SALMON FISHCAKES WITH PARSLEY SAUCE

Everybody should be able to make a good fishcake – mastering this sublime combination of fish and mashed potatoes arms you with one of the most versatile dishes around. It makes a perfect starter for a dinner party or I often have it for a yummy supper to nourish my soul.

Cook the potatoes in a pan of boiling salted water for 15–20 minutes until tender. Drain well and mash with half of the butter – you should have 250g (9oz) in total. Mix in the flaked hot smoked salmon, chives, baby capers and lemon juice and season generously, then mix well. Divide the mixture into four and then shape into patties. Place on a baking sheet, cover with cling film and chill in the fridge for at least 20 minutes but preferably 2 hours.

Place the flour on a shallow plate and put the breadcrumbs into a shallow dish. Break the eggs into a shallow bowl and lightly beat. Line everything up in a row. Dust the fishcakes lightly in the flour, then dip in the beaten egg and finally coat with the breadcrumbs.

To make the parsley sauce, pour boiling water over the parsley and leave to stand for 4 minutes. Drain well, then run under cold water until completely cooled. Squeeze out any excess water and blitz up with the olive oil in a mini food processor to form a very smooth purée.

Heat a little sunflower oil in a frying pan and add in the remaining butter. Add the fishcakes and fry for about 2–3 minutes on each side or until heated through and lightly golden. Drain well on kitchen paper.

To finish the parsley sauce, melt the butter in a pan and stir in the flour. Cook for at least 1 minute, stirring continuously, then stir in the mustard powder. Gradually pour in the milk, stirring until smooth after each addition until you have a lovely thick sauce. Fold in the parsley purée and season to taste, then cover with a piece of non-stick parchment paper and keep warm until you are ready to serve.

Serve the fishcakes with the parsley sauce and some wilted spinach, if you like. Garnish with a couple of lemon wedges.

350g (12oz) potatoes, cut into even-sized chunks
55g (2oz) unsalted butter
225g (8oz) hot smoked salmon, skinned and flaked into chunks
2 tbsp snipped fresh chives
1 tbsp baby capers, rinsed
1 tbsp fresh lemon juice
25g (1oz) seasoned plain flour
85g (3oz) fresh white breadcrumbs
2 eggs
sunflower oil, for frying
salt and freshly ground white pepper
wilted spinach, to serve (optional)
lemon wedges, to garnish

FOR THE PARSLEY SAUCE
25g (1oz) chopped fresh curly parsley
2 tbsp extra virgin olive oil
25g (1oz) butter
1 tbsp plain flour
1/2 tsp English mustard powder
200ml (7fl oz) milk

. . . .

Serves 4

PAILLARD OF SALMON WITH MUSHROOM RISOTTO

This is a wonderful autumnal dish and one that always sells in my restaurant. It's a great standby supper or lunch dish that needs little or no preparation. The trick of a good risotto is to add the stock little by little, allowing the liquid to be almost completely absorbed before adding the next ladleful.

1 tbsp olive oil
2 salmon fillets, skinned and cut across
    into thin slices
salt and freshly ground black pepper

FOR THE RISOTTO
2 tbsp olive oil
55g (2oz) butter
1 onion, finely chopped
2 garlic cloves, finely chopped
4 large flat mushrooms, diced
320g (11oz) risotto rice, such as Arborio
1 litre (1¾ pints) chicken stock
125ml (4fl oz) red wine
1 bay leaf
2 fresh thyme sprigs, leaves removed

FOR THE BAGNA CAUDA
225ml (8fl oz) olive oil
55g (2oz) butter, diced
55g can anchovies, drained and
    roughly chopped
4 garlic cloves, crushed

. . . .

Serves 4

To make the risotto, heat the olive oil and half of the butter in a large frying pan. Add the onion and garlic and cook for about 5 minutes until translucent. Stir in the mushrooms and fry for a further 2 minutes. Add the rice and cook for a few minutes until the grains start to turn slightly translucent.

Place the stock in a pan and bring to a gentle simmer. Pour the red wine into the rice mixture and simmer until all of the liquid has evaporated. Add the bay leaf and thyme leaves and stir well. Ladle in the hot stock, one ladle at a time, and only add more once it has all been absorbed. Stir continuously until all of the stock has been used and the rice is *al dente* and the risotto is creamy. Stir in the remaining butter.

Preheat the oven to 140C/275F/Gas 1 and preheat the grill. To make the *bagna cauda*, place the olive oil in a pan with the butter, anchovies and garlic and season to taste. Allow to warm through, but do not boil, until the anchovies have melted into the sauce.

To cook the salmon, lightly oil an ovenproof serving plate and place in the oven to warm. Arrange the slices of salmon on a sheet of cling film and cover with a second sheet. Pound out with a rolling pin until very flat. Transfer the paillards of salmon to the warm serving plate and drizzle over the remaining olive oil, then place under the grill for 1 minute until just cooked through.

Pour the *bagna cauda* over the plate of hot salmon and place directly on the table. Spoon the mushroom risotto into a warmed bowl and let everyone help themselves.

POACHED SALMON WITH DILL AND MUSTARD POTATOES

This recipe is a perfect example of how easy it is to cook restaurant-quality food in your own home. Wild salmon is preferable to farmed for this dish as the firmer flesh gives a better texture and stands up to the robust flavours in the poaching liquor.

Preheat the oven to 200C/400F/Gas 6. To prepare the poaching liquor, heat a frying pan. Add the coriander seeds, peppercorns, cardamom pods and star anise and heat for 2–3 minutes until aromatic. Tip into a pan that will hold the salmon fillets comfortably and pour in the olive oil. Warm gently for about 30 minutes to infuse with the wonderful flavours of the spices.

To start the dill and mustard potatoes, place the potatoes in a separate pan of salted water, then bring to the boil and cook for 10–15 minutes until tender.

Meanwhile, season the salmon fillets with salt and the cayenne pepper. Place the fennel in the centre of a piece of foil, then scatter over the garlic, thyme, star anise and wine. Season to taste and wrap into a parcel. Place on a baking sheet and cook in the oven for 20 minutes or until the fennel is completely soft and tender.

Carefully arrange the salmon fillets in the poaching liquor and simmer very gently for about 7 minutes or until the salmon is just tender but still pink in the middle. If you want to re-use the liquor then once it has cooled strain it and store in a cool, dark place.

To finish the dill and mustard potatoes, make the dressing. Place the crème fraîche in a bowl and stir in the wholegrain mustard, dill, lemon juice and horseradish. Season to taste. Drain the potatoes well and then stir in a spoonful of the dressing until lightly coated.

Arrange the dill and mustard potatoes on plates and put a piece of poached salmon on top. Spoon over the rest of the dill and mustard dressing and arrange the roasted fennel to the side to serve.

4 x 175g (6oz) salmon fillets, skinned and boned
¼ tsp cayenne pepper
12 baby fennel, trimmed
1 garlic clove, peeled
1 fresh thyme sprig
5g (⅛ oz) star anise
50ml (2fl oz) white wine
salt and freshly ground black pepper

FOR THE POACHING LIQUOR
10g (¼ oz) coriander seeds
10g (¼ oz) black peppercorns
10g (¼ oz) green cardamom pods
10g (¼ oz) star anise
1.5 litres (1¾ pints) olive oil

FOR THE DILL AND MUSTARD POTATOES
750g (1lb 10oz) small new potatoes, peeled
4 tbsp crème fraîche
1 tbsp wholegrain mustard
2 tbsp chopped fresh dill
juice of ½ lemon
1½ tsp freshly grated horseradish

Serves 4

SALMON IN FILO PASTRY WITH PERNOD SAUCE

This great looking dish is surprisingly easy to make and the results will surely impress your family, friends and guests. The sauce is also fairly simple to prepare, but has a sophisticated flavour that compliments the salmon perfectly.

175g (6oz) unsalted butter
55g (2oz) sultanas, chopped
8 x 85g (3oz) salmon fillets, skinned and pin bones removed (even-sized)
1 lemon
good handful of fresh mint leaves
16 filo pastry sheets, thawed if frozen
salt and freshly ground white pepper

FOR THE PERNOD SAUCE
knob butter
1 heaped tbsp plain flour
125ml (4fl oz) Pernod or pastis
2 egg yolks, beaten
1 tbsp chopped fresh mint

. . . .

Serves 4

Preheat the oven to 220C/425F/Gas 7. Melt 115g (4oz) of the butter and put to one side. Place four of the salmon fillets on the work surface and scatter over the sultanas. Cut the lemon into eight slices, discarding the ends and pips, then place on the sultanas. Scatter the mint leaves on top and season to taste. Place a knob of butter in the middle of each fillet. Place the four remaining fillets on the top to create a 'sandwich'.

Lay out a sheet of filo pastry and brush with the melted butter, then place the fillet 'sandwich' in the middle and neatly wrap with the pastry. Continue to wrap in buttered filo pastry until you have at least four layers of pastry to each parcel.

Brush the final pastry layer with melted butter and place the parcels on a baking sheet. Bake for 12–15 minutes until the pastry is golden brown and the salmon inside is cooked through and tender.

While the fish is in the oven, make the sauce. Melt the butter in a pan over a medium heat, add the flour and stir well until you have a smooth roux (paste). Cook the roux for a couple of minutes, stirring all the time, then whisk in the Pernod or pastis until you have a smooth sauce. Remove the pan from the heat and allow to cool a little, then whisk in the egg yolks until the sauce thickens. Add the mint and season to taste.

Pour the sauce onto warmed plates and top each one with a salmon in filo parcel to serve.

BALSAMIC-GLAZED TUNA WITH PARSLEY AND WALNUT SALSA AND RADISH SALAD

ANTONY WORRALL THOMPSON

I always encourage my restaurant customers to think of fresh tuna as a healthy alternative to fillet steak and to try it rare, but the choice is yours. Try to make this dish using small, young, spring radishes but if you get ones that are not as crisp as they should be, put them into a bowl of iced water and leave them for a couple of hours to firm up.

Preheat a griddle pan. Mix together the balsamic vinegar, sugar and garlic in a shallow non-metallic dish. Add the tuna, turning to coat and then leave to marinate for at least 5 and up to 15 minutes. Place the tuna on the heated griddle pan and cook for 1 minute on each side or longer if you prefer it more well done.

To make the parsley and walnut salsa, place the parsley in a food processor or liquidizer with the walnuts, lemon juice, garlic and olive oil. Pulse to chop roughly and then season to taste.

To make the radish salad, place the radishes in a bowl with the onion, basil, lemon juice and olive oil. Toss until well combined and season to taste.

Arrange piles of the radish salad on plates and top with the balsamic-glazed tuna steaks. Drizzle around the parsley and walnut salsa and serve at once.

4 tbsp balsamic vinegar
2 tbsp light muscovado sugar
1 garlic clove, finely chopped
4 x 175g (6oz) tuna steaks, each about 2.5cm (1 inch) thick
salt and freshly ground black pepper

FOR THE PARSLEY AND WALNUT SALSA
handful fresh flat-leaf parsley, roughly chopped
55g (2oz) walnuts, roughly chopped
juice of ½ lemon
1 garlic clove, roughly chopped
4 tbsp olive oil

FOR THE RADISH SALAD
140g (5oz) radishes, trimmed and sliced
1 small onion, sliced
handful fresh basil, roughly chopped
juice of ½ lemon
2 tbsp olive oil

Serves 4

CRAB AND PARMESAN TARTS

Made with the freshest white crab meat, a little brown meat, some Parmesan cheese and the shortest of pastry, this dish needs little accompaniment except a simple rocket salad and a chilled glass of Chablis. One large cooked brown crab should supply the right amount of crab meat for the tarts.

3 large eggs (preferably organic)
225g (8oz) white crab meat
55g (2oz) brown crab meat
200ml (7fl oz) crème fraîche
1 tbsp dry sherry
½ tsp mild cayenne pepper (or ¼ tsp hot cayenne pepper)
2 tbsp freshly grated Parmesan
85g (3oz) wild rocket
2 tbsp extra virgin olive oil
juice of ½ lemon
salt and freshly ground black pepper

FOR THE PASTRY:
300g (10½ oz) plain flour
200g (7oz) ricotta cheese

. . . .

Serves 4

To make the pastry, mix together the flour, ricotta and a pinch of salt in a bowl and knead, adding a little water to soften as you go, until you have a smooth, soft dough. Wrap in cling film and leave to rest in the fridge for 20 minutes.

Roll out the pastry on a lightly floured board to a 3mm (⅛ inch) thickness and use to line 4 x 12cm (4½ inch) individual flan tins that are at least 2.5cm (1 inch) deep. Return to the fridge to allow the pastry to rest for another 20 minutes or so.

Meanwhile, preheat the oven to 180C/350F/Gas 4. Beat the eggs in a bowl and add the crab meat. Stir in the crème fraîche, sherry, cayenne, and 4 teaspoons of the Parmesan.

Prick the pastry bases with a fork, then line each one with a circle of non-stick baking paper or foil that is first crumpled up to make it easier to handle. Fill with ceramic baking beans or dried pulses. Sit the flan tins on a baking tray and bake for about 10 minutes until the cases look 'set'.

Carefully remove the paper or foil and the beans from the pastry case.

Season the crab mixture and divide evenly among the pastry cases. Sprinkle over the remaining Parmesan and place in the oven for 15–20 minutes until the crab filling is just set and lightly golden. Allow to cool slightly.

Meanwhile, place the rocket in a large bowl and toss with the olive oil and lemon juice. Season to taste

Arrange the crab and Parmesan tarts on plates with small mounds of the dressed rocket salad on the side to serve.

TUNA AND SUN-DRIED TOMATO FISHCAKES

These fishcakes have plenty of gutsy flavours and they're served with some blanched beans and quite a sharp dressing to cut through the richness of the dish. Kids will love them and they are a fantastic way of getting children to eat fish.

225g (8oz) potatoes, cut into
    even-sized chunks

200g can cannellini beans,
    drained and rinsed

1 egg

400g can tuna chunks in olive
    oil, drained

115g (4oz) sun-dried tomatoes in oil,
    drained and chopped

1 garlic clove, finely chopped

4 tbsp chopped fresh flat-leaf parsley

finely grated rind of 1 lemon

squeeze of lemon juice

175g (6oz) toasted fine white
    breadcrumbs

salt and freshly ground black pepper

FOR THE GREEN BEANS

200g (7oz) green beans, trimmed

1 tbsp extra virgin olive oil

squeeze of lemon juice

. . . .

Serves 4

Preheat the oven to 180C/350F/Gas 4. Cook the potatoes in a pan of boiling salted water for 15–20 minutes until tender. Drain and mash well.

Lightly mash the cannellini beans in a large bowl and add the mashed potato, mixing well to combine. Add the egg, tuna, sun-dried tomatoes, garlic and parsley and mix together well. Season to taste, then stir in the lemon rind and juice.

If you find the mixture is too wet, add some of the toasted breadcrumbs until you get a firmer consistency. Then use your hands to make medium-size balls and flatten them gently. Place the toasted breadcrumbs in a shallow dish and use to coat the fishcakes.

Place the fishcakes on a baking sheet lined with non-stick parchment paper and bake for approximately 15 minutes until heated through and crunchy on the outside.

Meanwhile, prepare the green beans. Cook the beans in a pan of salted boiling water for 2–3 minutes until *al dente*. Drain well and tip in a large bowl. Toss with extra virgin olive oil and a squeeze of lemon juice, and season with salt.

Arrange the fishcakes on warmed plates and serve with the crunchy green beans.

SPAGHETTI WITH SEARED SCALLOPS

Look for plump, firm, moist scallops with a sweet aroma. Avoid scallops that are bright white as they have been soaked in water or brine to make them swell up and appear larger. Unsoaked scallops should be a lovely creamy or slightly off-white colour.

Cook the spaghetti in a large pan of salted boiling water for 8–10 minutes, or according to packet instructions, until *al dente*.

Meanwhile, heat 1 tbsp olive oil in a heavy-based frying pan. When it is hot, add the bacon, mushrooms and garlic. Fry until the mushrooms are browned and the bacon is cooked through.

In a bowl, whisk the egg yolks, double cream, Parmesan cheese, parsley, basil and chilli with a pinch of salt and pepper.

When the spaghetti is cooked, drain well. While the pasta is still hot, add the bacon and mushrooms along with the egg and cream mixture. Stir well so everything gets a good coating.

Meanwhile, add the remaining olive oil to a hot pan and sear the scallops for 2 minutes on each side, until cooked.

To serve, spoon some spaghetti onto warmed plates and place 5 scallops per person on top.

500g packet of spaghetti
2 tbsp olive oil
8 rashers streaky bacon, diced
2 portobello mushrooms, finely sliced
2 garlic cloves, sliced
2 egg yolks
6 tbsp double cream
115g (4oz) Parmesan cheese, finely grated
2 tbsp finely chopped parsley
4 tbsp torn basil leaves
½ tsp medium-hot chilli powder
20 scallops
salt and freshly ground black pepper

. . . .

Serves 4

LINGUINE WITH PRAWNS AND ROCKET

The supreme strength of Italian cuisine is that the unique flavours of the ingredients are presented in such a way that they enhance, but do not smother, each other. All the flavours in this pasta dish are interesting on their own, but together they are stunning.

Cook the pasta in a large pan of salted boiling water for 8–10 minutes, or according to packet instructions, until *al dente*.

Heat the olive oil in a large frying pan and fry the garlic and chilli for about 20 seconds, stirring frequently. Add the prawns and cook for a further minute. Add the wine and basil and season with salt, then simmer gently for another 2 minutes or until the prawns are cooked through.

Drain the pasta and return to the pan. Add the prawn sauce and immediately tip in the rocket leaves. Mix well on a low heat, allowing the rocket leaves to soften slightly and the pasta to absorb the flavours.

Spoon the linguine with prawns and rocket into warmed wide-rimmed bowls to serve.

500g packet linguine

5 tbsp olive oil

1 garlic clove, finely sliced

1 medium red chilli, finely sliced

300g (10½ oz) large raw prawns, peeled, de-veined and head and tails removed

50ml (2fl oz) dry white wine

3 tbsp finely shredded fresh basil

115g (4oz) rocket

pinch of salt

. . . .

Serves 4

PRAWN CURRY WITH CARDAMOM-SCENTED BASMATI RICE

King prawns are now being farmed with great success. They are easy to find and you should be able to get all of the ingredients to make this dish at most large supermarkets or an Oriental food shop.

1 tbsp olive oil

300g (10½ oz) raw king prawns, shelled and de-veined

115g (4oz) shiitake mushrooms, stalks removed and finely sliced

120ml (4fl oz) chicken stock

200g (7oz) coconut milk

1 lemon grass stick, well trimmed and finely chopped

15g (½ oz) freshly grated root ginger

2 garlic cloves, crushed

good pinch curry powder

juice of 1 lemon

2 tbsp chopped fresh coriander

salt and freshly ground black pepper

FOR THE SCENTED BASMATI RICE

2 tbsp olive oil

500g (1lb 2oz) long grain rice

4 cardamom pods, cracked

6 fenugreek seeds

good pinch black onion seeds

2 chicken stock cubes, crumbled

2 kaffir lime leaves

. . . .

Serves 4

Preheat the oven to 220C/425F/Gas 7. To prepare the rice, heat the olive oil in an ovenproof pan with a lid and toss in the rice, cardamom pods, fenugreek seeds and onion seeds. Add the stock cubes and lime leaves and then pour in 1.2 litres (2 pints) of cold water. Stir well to combine, put on the lid and place in the oven for 20–25 minutes until all of the liquid has been absorbed.

To make the curry, heat the olive oil in a large pan. Add the prawns and shiitake mushrooms and stir fry for 1–2 minutes until cooked through and lightly golden. Tip into a bowl and set aside.

Add the stock and coconut milk to the pan over a gentle heat. Add the lemon grass and ginger and gently heat through. Season to taste and add the garlic, then allow to reduce for a couple of minutes, stirring occasionally.

Sprinkle the curry powder into the reduced coconut milk mixture and allow to cook for 1–2 minutes, stirring occasionally. Bring to a simmer and add the lemon juice. Stir well to combine and remove from the heat.

Return the prawns and shiitake mushrooms to the curry and bring to a gentle simmer to just heat through.

Stir the cooked rice with a fork to fluff it up and spoon onto warmed plates, then ladle over the prawn curry and sprinkle with the coriander to serve.

BOOZY PRAWN STIR-FRY

This is a *Meals on Reels* recipe. The whisky was a quite a challenge but it works surprisingly well. The dish is full of fantastic zingy and spicy flavours and packs quite a punch.

To prepare the noodles, drop them into a pan of boiling water and remove from the heat. Stir with a fork and leave to stand for 4 minutes or according to packet instructions.

While the noodles are cooking, heat the vegetable oil in a wok until hot. Add the garlic and stir-fry for 10–20 seconds until golden, then add in the spring onions and cook for a further minute.

Add the chilli flakes to the spring onion mixture with the salt and pepper and the prawns and cook for a minute or two until the prawns have turned pink and are cooked through.

Sprinkle over the whisky and then burn off the alcohol. Add the soy and honey and stir through the coriander.

Drain the noodles and toss with the sesame oil, soy sauce and coriander. Divide among warmed plates and spoon the boozy prawns on top.

2 tbsp vegetable oil

2 garlic cloves, thinly sliced

2 bunches spring onions, cut into 2.5cm (1 inch) pieces on the diagonal

2 tsp dried chilli flakes

½ tsp salt

1 tsp cracked black pepper

500g (1lb 2oz) raw king prawns, shelled and de-veined

4 tbsp whisky

2 tbsp soy sauce

2 tsp honey

bunch fresh coriander, roughly chopped

FOR THE NOODLES

400g packet egg noodles

2 tsp toasted sesame oil

2 tbsp soy sauce

handful fresh coriander, roughly chopped

. . . .

Serves 4

PRAWNS WITH CHORIZO AND SHERRY

Bring a touch of Spain to your kitchen! You can knock up this delicious tapas dish in about 5 minutes flat.

2 tbsp olive oil
300g (10¹/₂ oz) chorizo sausage, cut into
    bite-size chunks
20 raw, peeled tiger prawns
¹/₂ red chilli, seeded and finely chopped
1 garlic clove, crushed
100ml (3¹/₂ fl oz) dry sherry
squeeze of lemon juice
2 tbsp fresh flat-leaf parsley,
    roughly chopped
salt and freshly ground black pepper
crusty bread, to serve

. . . .

Serves 4

Heat the olive oil in a frying pan. Add the chorizo and fry for about 30 seconds until the bright red oil is starting to melt from the sausage.

Add the prawns to the pan and fry until they are slightly golden on both sides. Stir in the chilli and garlic and then pour over the sherry. Season to taste and cook over a high heat for about 3 minutes. Squeeze in the lemon juice and scatter over the parsley.

Divide the prawns with chorizo and sherry among warmed plates or shallow dishes. Serve with crusty bread to mop up the juices.

CURRIED MOULES MARINIERES EN PAPILLOTE

These aromatic mussels can also be baked in squares of non-stick parchment paper. Simply cut out 38cm (15 inch) squares and crumple them into small balls, then open them out again. Pile in the mussel mixture and then lift up opposite sides of each paper square and fold together, twisting and tucking in the ends to form a secure parcel.

2 tbsp olive oil

2 large onions, chopped

12 garlic cloves, crushed

bunch fresh flat-leaf parsley, leaves stripped and chopped

2kg (4lb 8oz) mussels, well cleaned and beards removed (discard any that fail to close when tapped against the side of the sink)

200ml (7fl oz) white wine

2 tbsp curry powder

175g (6oz) crème fraîche

800g (1lb 12oz) purple sprouting broccoli, chopped

salt and freshly ground black pepper

. . . .

Serves 4

Preheat the oven to 200C/400F/Gas 6. Heat the olive oil in a large pan and sweat the onions with three of the garlic cloves, the parsley and some seasoning for about 5 minutes until soft and transparent.

Add the mussels to the pan, tossing to combine. When they start to open, pour in the white wine and sprinkle over the curry powder and the remaining garlic cloves. Toss vigorously until well mixed, then remove from the heat.

Line four ovenproof bowls with tin foil and divide the mussels among them, reserving the liquor. Spoon over the crème fraiche and then close the foil. Arrange the bowls on baking sheets and cook for 4 minutes or until all of the mussels have opened; discard any that do not.

Meanwhile, bring the remaining mussel juices to a simmer and tip in the purple sprouting broccoli. Stir-fry for 2 minutes until just tender but still crunchy. Season to taste.

Arrange the broccoli in warmed wide-rimmed bowls and spoon over the curried moules marinière to serve.

HERRING FILLETS WITH PICKLED APPLE

When buying herrings, freshness is the most important quality to look for, so buy from a reliable fishmonger. As herring is quite an oily fish it tastes best on the day it's caught. If you're lucky enough to get it spanking fresh, I promise you'll understand what all the fuss is about.

Preheat the oven to 180C/350F/Gas 4. To make the pickled apple, melt the butter in a frying pan. Add the onion, apple and celery and cook for a few minutes to colour slightly.

Add the cider to the apple mixture with the cider vinegar and honey, then cook slowly for 20 minutes, stirring occasionally, until all of the liquid has evaporated. Season to taste.

Trim the herring fillets and lay them in an ovenproof dish. Cover with the cider and fish stock and bake for 15 minutes or until cooked through and tender.

Take the cooked herrings out of the oven and transfer to a warmed plate, cover with foil and set to one side. Keep warm.

Pour the cooking liquor into a pan and reduce by half. Beat in the butter, add the parsley and season to taste.

Arrange the herring fillets on warmed plates and spoon the pickled apple to the side. Pour around the cider sauce and serve at once with crusty bread.

12 herring fillets
125ml (4fl oz) dry cider
150ml (¼ pint) fish stock
55g (2oz) butter, diced and chilled
2 tbsp chopped fresh flat-leaf parsley
salt and freshly ground black pepper
crusty bread, to serve

FOR THE PICKLED APPLE
25g (1oz) butter
1 red onion, finely chopped
1 green apple, peeled, cored and diced
1 celery stick, diced
2 tbsp cider
2 tbsp cider vinegar
1 tsp runny honey

....

Serves 4

vegetarian

MELANZANE ALLA PARMIGIANA

A very tasty dish for vegetarians that is really rather filling. I like to serve it with some warm griddled ciabatta bread that has been drizzled with olive oil but it's also excellent with a lightly dressed rocket salad.

Place the aubergine slices in a large colander. Sprinkle with salt and set aside for 30 minutes in the sink to allow the excess liquid to drain off.

Heat 5 tablespoons of the olive oil in a large pan and gently fry the onion, celery and carrot for about 5 minutes until soft. Add the chopped tomatoes, season to taste and cook for about 10 minutes until slightly reduced and thickened. Leave to cool.

Remove the aubergines from the sieve, place them on a kitchen towel and pat dry.

Preheat the oven to 180C/350F/Gas 4. Heat the remaining olive oil in a large frying pan. Place the flour onto a flat plate. Tip the eggs in a bowl, season to taste and lightly beat. Dust the aubergines in the flour, then dip in the beaten egg and fry until golden on both sides. Place on some kitchen paper to drain off any excess oil.

Cover the bottom of a large ovenproof dish with some of the aubergine slices. Spread some of the cooled tomato sauce over the aubergine, then place some mozzarella slices on top. Sprinkle over some of the Parmesan and basil leaves. Repeat the process three times.

Finally, spread the remaining tomato sauce on top, sprinkle over the remaining Parmesan, cover with foil and bake in the oven for 20 minutes.

Remove the foil and continue to bake for a further 30 minutes until bubbling and lightly golden.

Leave to rest for 5 minutes, then carefully cut into portions and arrange on warmed plates. Hand around warm griddled ciabatta bread to serve.

6 large aubergines, cut into 1cm (½ inch) slices
150ml (¼ pint) olive oil
1 onion, finely chopped
2 celery sticks, finely chopped
1 large carrot, finely chopped
4 x 400g cans chopped tomatoes
200g (7oz) plain flour
4 eggs
3 mozzarella balls, drained and sliced
200g (7oz) freshly grated Parmesan
20 fresh basil leaves
salt and freshly ground black pepper
griddled warm ciabatta slices drizzled with olive oil, to serve

Serves 4–6

ASPARAGUS AND GOATS' CHEESE TART

These tarts celebrate the coming of spring by using British asparagus, which is in season for roughly eight weeks in May and June. Perfect for a light supper, especially with a tomato salad or try a raw fennel, watercress and walnut salad as a refreshing alternative.

500g packet ready-made puff pastry, thawed if frozen
a little plain flour, for dusting
16 asparagus spears, trimmed
a little olive oil, for greasing
85g (3oz) goats' cheese, crumbled
50g (1¾oz) mascarpone cheese
100ml (3½ fl oz) tbsp double cream
1 garlic clove, finely chopped
3 sun-dried tomatoes, finely chopped
1 egg, beaten
salt and freshly ground black pepper

. . . .

Serves 4

Roll out the pastry on a lightly floured board to a 5mm (¼ inch) thickness. Cut into four even-sized rectangles, each about 10cm x 15cm (4 x 6 inches), and trim the edges. Arrange on large greased baking sheets; score a 1cm (¼ inch) border around the edge of the pastry rectangles and prick the insides with a fork. Chill for at least 30 minutes.

Preheat the oven to 200C/400F/Gas 6. Blanch the asparagus spears in a pan of boiling water for 2 minutes. Drain well and refresh quickly under cold running water.

Mix the goats' cheese in a bowl with the mascarpone, double cream and garlic, then season to taste. Spread over the pastry bases, keeping inside the scored border, and arrange the asparagus on top to cover the goats' cheese mixture completely. Sprinkle over the sun-dried tomatoes. Brush the pastry borders with the beaten egg. Season to taste and bake for 12–15 minutes or until the pastry is puffed up and golden brown.

Remove the tarts from the oven and transfer to warmed plates to serve.

ANTONY WORRALL THOMPSON

ANTONY WORRALL THOMPSON

WATERCRESS SOUFFLE

Contrary to popular belief soufflés are not difficult to make: just use the freshest eggs you can get hold of to ensure a perfect rise. This one has a wonderful light, moist texture and the watercress flavour comes bursting through.

Preheat the oven to 200C/400F/Gas 6. Melt the butter in a small pan, then stir in the flour and cook the roux gently for 2–3 minutes, stirring constantly.

Warm the milk in a separate pan and then gradually add to the roux, a little at a time, stirring until smooth after each addition. Bring to the boil, stirring constantly. Remember to scrape round the edges of the pan so that all the uncooked roux is well stirred in.

When the mixture comes to the boil, let it simmer over a very gentle heat for 3–5 minutes, stirring occasionally. Then remove the pan from the heat and add the Cheddar and mustard. Leave to cool a little.

Separate the eggs, then beat the egg yolks into the cooled cheese sauce and season to taste – remember that the cheese will already have made this sauce quite salty. Stir in the watercress and set aside.

Beat the egg whites in a china, glass or copper bowl, preferably with a hand whisk, until they are moist and velvet in appearance and just peak softly. Then stir a spoonful of beaten egg white into the cooked sauce. Fold in the remaining egg whites in two batches, cutting the mixture through with a metal spoon or palette knife.

Pour the mixture immediately into a greased 850ml (1½ pint) soufflé dish and bake in the middle of the oven for 25 minutes or until it's well risen and firm to the touch in the centre.

Serve the watercress soufflé straight away and allow everyone to help themselves.

25g (1oz) butter, plus extra for greasing
25g (1oz) plain flour
300ml (½ pint) milk
55g (2oz) Cheddar, grated
¼ tsp prepared English mustard
4 eggs
1 bunch watercress, well picked over and very finely chopped
salt and freshly ground black pepper

....

Serves 4

CARAMELIZED BEETROOT ON SPINACH AND YOGHURT

Beetroot seems to get forgotten about all too often but I love it, especially when roasted until tender. Try this recipe as a nice vegetarian starter, or serve it with slices of rare roast beef for the meat lovers among us.

12 baby beetroots, peeled and
   well trimmed
1 tbsp olive oil
2 tbsp balsamic vinegar
55g (2oz) butter
2 shallots, finely chopped
4 handfuls baby spinach leaves
2 tbsp Greek strained yoghurt
1 tbsp chopped fresh flat-leaf parsley
salt and freshly ground black pepper

. . . .

Serves 4

Preheat the oven to 200C/400F/Gas 6. Put the beetroot into a small roasting dish with olive oil. Season with salt and roast in the oven for about 10 minutes.

Remove the beetroots from the oven and sprinkle over the balsamic vinegar, then place directly on the stove top and cook for a few minutes until the beetroot is caramelized, shaking the roasting tin occasionally.

Melt the butter in a pan and add the shallots, then cook for 3–4 minutes until softened but not coloured. Stir in the spinach, and cook until it starts to wilt. Drain off any excess liquid, then fold in the yoghurt and season to taste.

Spoon the spinach mixture into the centre of each warmed plate and top with three caramelized beetroots. Sprinkle over the parsley to serve.

CHEESY NACHOS WITH GUACAMOLE AND SALSA

The perfect late night snack after a couple of pints. Mexican restaurants and cinemas charge loads for a plate of nachos but they're quite inexpensive to make at home. Have a go yourself and you'll see how easy and tasty they really are.

225g bag plain tortilla chips
200g (7oz) mature Cheddar, grated
salt and freshly ground black pepper

FOR THE GUACAMOLE
4 large ripe avocados, halved, stoned, peeled and cut in cubes
2 tsp garlic purée
1/2 tsp paprika
juice of 2 limes
25g (1oz) sliced jalapeño chillies (from a jar), finely chopped
1 tbsp chopped fresh coriander

FOR THE SALSA
1 tbsp olive oil
350g can sweetcorn, drained
1 tbsp light muscovado sugar
1 tbsp sherry vinegar
140g (5oz) cherry tomatoes, quartered
2 large spring onions, finely chopped
1 red chilli, halved, seeded and finely chopped
85ml (3fl oz) soured cream
1 tbsp chopped fresh flat-leaf parsley
1 tbsp chopped fresh coriander

To make the guacamole, tip the avocado into a large bowl and add the garlic purée, paprika and lime juice. Using a fork, mash everything together, creating a semi-smooth texture. Fold in the jalapeño chillies with the coriander and season to taste. Transfer to a bowl, cover with cling film and chill until needed.

To make the salsa, heat a frying pan and, once hot, add the olive oil. Tip in the sweetcorn and fry for a few minutes until it begins to colour. Remove from the heat and sprinkle over the sugar and vinegar, mixing well to combine. Leave to cool, then place in a bowl. Stir in the cherry tomatoes, spring onions, chilli, soured cream, parsley and coriander. Season to taste.

Preheat the grill until hot. Pile up the tortilla chips on a large ovenproof platter. Scatter over the Cheddar and season with black pepper. Place under the grill for a few minutes or until the cheese is bubbling and golden.

Serve the cheesy nachos with the bowls of guacamole and salsa for dipping.

Serves 2–4

HOME-STYLE FRIED EGGS

This is one of my favourite snacks. The eggs are crispy and chewy at the same time. I love them drizzled with oyster sauce – a thick, brown condiment made from a concentrate of oysters cooked in soy sauce and brine. Once it's opened it's best kept in the refrigerator.

Heat the oil in a wok until the surface seems to shimmer slightly. Crack each egg into a small bowl, then carefully pour into the hot oil. After 1 minute reduce the heat to medium allowing the underside of the eggs to become firm and crisp.

While the yolks are still runny, transfer them to a plate with an fish slice, then pour off and discard the oil. Return the eggs to the wok and cook for a another minute to crisp up further. Gently remove the eggs from the wok and drain off any excess oil on kitchen paper.

Place the eggs on warmed plates and drizzle over the oyster sauce. Season with the white pepper and scatter over the chilli and spring onions to serve.

350ml (12fl oz) vegetable oil
4 eggs (organic, if possible)
1 tbsp oyster sauce
good pinch ground white pepper
1 birds eye chilli, finely sliced
4 spring onions, finely sliced

. . . .

Serves 2–4

COURGETTE AND LEMON PASTA WITH PARMESAN

ANTONY WORRALL THOMPSON

It's hard to believe that the word spaghetti, as the description of a type of pasta, has only officially been in existence since 1836 when it was recorded in an Italian dialect dictionary for the region of Piacenza. Perhaps this was because until the introduction of powerful pasta machines in the latter part of the 19th century, its production was a laborious business.

225g (8oz) spaghetti
450g (1lb) courgettes, coarsely grated
4 tbsp olive oil
55g (2oz) pine nuts, toasted
finely grated rind and juice of 1 lemon
200g (7oz) freshly grated Parmesan
good pinch dried chilli flakes
salt and freshly ground black pepper

. . . .

Serves 4

Bring a large pan of water to a rolling boil. Swirl in the spaghetti and cook for 10-12 minutes until *al dente* or according to packet instructions.

Meanwhile, heat a large frying pan. Put the courgettes in a clean tea towel and squeeze dry. Add the olive oil to the frying pan and quickly fry the courgettes for about 5 minutes until tender and just beginning to colour around the edges.

Add the pine nuts to the courgettes with the lemon rind and plenty of black pepper and continue to fry for another minute or so.

Drain the spaghetti and add to the pan with the courgette and pine nut mixture. Add most of the Parmesan and the chilli flakes and toss until well combined. Season and add lemon juice to taste.

Divide the courgette and lemon pasta among warmed wide-rimmed bowls and sprinkle over the remaining Parmesan to serve.

TRENETTE AL PESTO

In Italy we use different pasta for different sauces but this has to be the most classic combination of all. It brings back memories of when I worked the summer season in hotels in the Costa Ligure near Genoa, which is where pesto is originally from. Of course, you can use a food processor instead of a pestle and mortar but the result is not quite as spectacular.

400g packet trenette pasta

FOR THE PESTO
35g (1 1/4 oz) fresh basil leaves
2 tbsp toasted pine nuts
2 garlic cloves, peeled
25g (1oz) freshly grated Parmesan
75g (3oz) freshly grated Pecorino
250ml (9fl oz) extra virgin olive oil
splash cold sparkling water (optional)
salt and freshly ground black pepper

....

Serves 4

To make the pesto, clean the basil leaves with a damp cloth if necessary and then place in a pestle and mortar. Add the pine nuts, garlic and some seasoning and start slowly working the ingredients together.

Add the Parmesan to the basil mixture with the Pecorino and olive oil. Carry on grinding until you achieve a paste. Thin down with the sparkling water if you think it needs it. If keeping for a while, cover the pesto with olive oil to keep it fresh and store in the fridge.

When ready to cook, bring a large pot of salted water to the boil. Tip in the pasta, give it a good stir and cook for 8–10 minutes until *al dente* or according to the instructions on the packet.

Drain the pasta and stir in the pesto sauce, allowing it to warm through. Divide among wide-rimmed bowls and serve at once.

DEEP-FRIED POLENTA

Polenta is cornmeal porridge and at first taste is about as attractive as it sounds. However, there are ways of making it more edible: namely with plenty of good olive oil and lots of grated Pecorino. Just be careful when you are stirring it, as the mixture tends to imitate boiling volcanic mud as large bubbles surface and explode messily.

Generously butter a 20cm (8 inch) baking dish and set aside. Bring 750ml (26fl oz) of water to the boil, season with salt and then pour in the polenta in a steady stream, stirring vigorously with a wooden spoon in your other hand.

Turn the heat to medium and stir the polenta until it boils. Now reduce the heat to low and simmer for 5 minutes or according to packet instructions.

Meanwhile, heat the olive oil in a large frying pan and gently fry the onions and sage for about 5 minutes until lightly golden, stirring occasionally.

Remove the cooked polenta from the heat and stir in the onion and sage mixture with the Pecorino cheese and season to taste. Pour into the buttered dish; it should be a minimum of 2cm (¾ inch) deep. Bang the baking dish gently on the work surface to level and allow to cool completely.

Once cooled, tip the polenta onto a chopping board and cut into thick slices. Heat the vegetable oil in a deep-fat fryer to 190C/375F or use a deep-sided pan and cook the polenta slices in batches for about 1 minute until crisp and lightly golden. Drain well on kitchen paper.

Arrange the deep-fried polenta slices on plates with the mixed salad to serve.

good knob butter
250g (9oz) instant polenta
5 tbsp olive oil
2 onions, finely chopped
6 fresh sage leaves, shredded
**115g (4oz) freshly grated
  Pecorino cheese**
vegetable oil, for deep-frying
salt
lightly dressed mixed salad, to serve

. . . .

Serves 4

light bites

FRENCH ONION SOUP

No two recipes for this soup are ever the same, however all agree that it should be thick with gently cooked onions that have coloured the broth a deep chestnut-brown. I prefer my bread croûtons to retain some of their crunchiness and I like the cheese to be thoroughly molten and crusty. To achieve this it's important that the bread is hard to start with.

Melt the butter in a large pan and cook the onions for about 6–8 minutes until softened, stirring occasionally. Add the sugar and cook for a further 5 minutes until the onions begin to caramelize.

Pour the white wine into the pan and allow to bubble down, then add the chicken stock and cook for 5 minutes until reduced. Stir in the vegetable stock and add the thyme and bay leaf, then simmer for 20 minutes, stirring occasionally. Season to taste.

Meanwhile, make the croûtons. Preheat the grill. Cut the baguette into thick slices and brush with the garlic oil, then scatter over the cheese. Arrange on a grill rack and cook for 2–3 minutes until the cheese is bubbling and golden.

Ladle the French onion soup into bowls and top with the cheesy croûtons to serve.

115g (4oz) unsalted butter

600g (1lb 5oz) red onions, halved and thinly sliced

1 tsp sugar

125ml (4fl oz) dry white wine

100ml (3 1/2 fl oz) chicken stock

1 litre (1 3/4 pints) vegetable stock

1 small fresh thyme sprig

1 bay leaf

salt and freshly ground black pepper

FOR THE CROUTONS

1 small baguette

2 tbsp garlic oil

85g (3oz) Gruyère cheese, grated

. . . .

Serves 4

BROAD BEAN AND FETA DIP

This makes a can of broad beans go a long way. It may seem like a complete bore to slip them out of their white papery skins but it's absolutely worth the effort. I like to serve this with Lebanese or Moroccan flatbreads but it's also great with a selection of crudités, depending on what you have to hand.

300g can broad beans, drained
    and rinsed
200g (7oz) feta cheese
1 sprig fresh mint
juice of 1 lemon
1 tbsp Greek strained yoghurt (optional)
salt and freshly ground black pepper
pitta bread, to serve

Pop the broad beans out of their skins and place in a food processor or liquidizer. Add the feta, mint and lemon juice and blend to a smooth paste. If the mixture is too thick, add the Greek yoghurt to loosen it a little. Season to taste and transfer to a bowl.

Set the bowl of broad bean and feta dip on a plate and pile pieces of the pitta bread to the side to serve.

. . . .

Serves 4

ANTONY WORRALL THOMPSON

STEAMED ASPARAGUS WITH HERB PANGRATTATO

ANTONY WORRALL THOMPSON

Pangrattato gives this dish an excellent texture and crunch. It is basically fried or toasted breadcrumbs in garlic oil. Traditionally it was used in Italy instead of Parmesan and when well made it's completely delicious. Try to find small tender asparagus spears for a full sweet flavour and delicate taste.

To make the pangrattato, cover the eggs with water and bring to a simmer, then cook for 8–10 minutes until hard boiled. Drain and rinse under cold running water. Once cool enough to handle, crack away the shells and chop up. Set aside.

Cut the bottom crust off the ciabatta loaf and discard. Cut the remainder into rough cubes and then blitz into coarse breadcrumbs in a food processor or liquidizer.

Heat the oil in a small pan and add the whole garlic cloves. Cook gently over a low heat for 8–10 minutes or until they are a deep golden colour, then remove and discard. Add the breadcrumbs and cook for a few minutes until golden, tossing the pan occasionally.

Just as the breadcrumbs begin to turn brown, add the herbs, lemon rind and chopped hard-boiled eggs. Immediately remove the breadcrumb mixture from the oil using a slotted spoon, and drain on kitchen paper. Season to taste.

Meanwhile, cook the asparagus for 3–6 minutes, depending on the size of the spears, in a large pan of boiling salted water or in a steamer standing in 7.5cm (3 inches) of boiling water until just tender. Drain and quickly refresh under cold running water.

Arrange the cooked asparagus on warmed plates and sprinkle over the pangrattato to serve.

20–24 small asparagus spears, trimmed
salt and freshly ground black pepper

FOR THE HERB PANGRATTATO
2 eggs
1 ciabatta loaf
200ml (7fl oz) extra virgin olive oil
6 garlic cloves, peeled
1 tbsp chopped fresh thyme
1 tbsp chopped fresh rosemary
finely grated rind of 1 lemon

....

Serves 4

SPICED MACKEREL WITH VEGETABLE RAITA

This is a fabulous way of cooking mackerel on a barbecue. Of course you could do them in a pan but they'll never taste quite as good. It's a great recipe to prepare in advance and come back to once you've lit the coals.

8 x 85g (3oz) mackerel fillets
salt and freshly ground black pepper

FOR THE SPICE PASTE
1 tbsp coriander seeds
1 tbsp black mustard seeds
1 tbsp cumin seeds
1 tsp black peppercorns
1 dried hot chilli, roughly chopped, seeded if wished
1 tsp salt
1 tbsp dark muscovado sugar

FOR THE VEGETABLE RAITA
1 cucumber, peeled, halved, seeded and diced
1 plum tomato, seeded and diced
1 small red onion, very finely chopped
1 cooked potato, peeled and diced
1/2 tsp toasted cumin seeds
425ml (15fl oz) Greek strained yogurt
1 tbsp chopped fresh mint

. . . .

Serves 4

To make the spice paste, heat a dry frying pan over a medium heat then add the coriander, black mustard seeds, cumin seeds and the black peppercorns and toast for 2–3 minutes, shaking from time to time until the mustard seeds are popping and the spices are aromatic. (You may need to cover the frying pan to stop the mustard seeds jumping out.)

Blend the toasted spices with the chilli to a smooth powder in a coffee grinder or with a pestle and mortar. Combine the spice powder with the salt and sugar. Store in an airtight container until needed.

To make the vegetable raita, place the cucumber in a bowl with the tomato, onion, potato and cumin seeds. Stir in the Greek yoghurt and mint, then season to taste. Cover with cling film and chill until needed. It will keep happily in the fridge for up to two days.

Half an hour before cooking the fish, lightly sprinkle both sides of each mackerel fillet with the spice mixture – about two teaspoons per fillet. Store any remaining spice mixture for future use.

Place the fillets in a metal hinged rack and cook on a hot barbecue for 1–2 minutes on each side until lightly charred and firm to the touch. Or cook the mackerel fillets in a hot griddle pan for a few minutes on each side, until cooked through and tender

Arrange the spiced mackerel fillets on plates and spoon the vegetable raita on the side to serve.

PRAWN AND COCONUT SATAY BROTH

This is what I make if I'm looking for a bit of comfort after a long day at work. It's fragrant with a touch of heat but also delicious and sweet with the background flavour of coconut.

225g (8oz) medium egg noodles

2 tbsp vegetable oil

2 garlic cloves, crushed

1 red chilli, halved, seeded and finely sliced

2 tbsp smooth or crunchy peanut butter

400g can coconut milk

1 litre (1 3/4 pints) chicken or vegetable stock

400g (14oz) cooked king prawns, thawed if frozen

2 bunches spring onions, thinly sliced

2 tsp soy sauce

1/2 lime, pips removed

good handful fresh coriander, roughly chopped

. . . .

Serves 4

Plunge the noodles into a pan of boiling water. Remove from the heat and set aside for 4 minutes until tender or according to packet instructions. Drain well.

Meanwhile, heat a large wok or pan until hot. Add the oil and then tip in the garlic and chilli. Stir fry for 10–20 seconds, then add the peanut butter and coconut milk and stir to make a loose paste.

Pour the stock into the coconut mixture and bring to a simmer. Add the prawns, spring onions and soy sauce and simmer for 2–3 minutes until the prawns are heated through.

Tip the cooked noodles into the prawn mixture and return to a simmer. Squeeze in the lime juice and scatter over coriander, then divide among warmed bowls to serve.

TUNA AND BEAN SALAD ON CIABATTA

This salad should be served at room temperature. It's success completely depends on the quality of the ingredients. It also makes excellent picnic food or a valuable addition to an antipasti platter for a spur of the moment nibble.

Place the cannellini beans in a bowl and add the spring onions, tuna and half of the olive oil. Mix well to combine, then squeeze over the lemon juice and scatter the parsley on top. Season to taste. Set aside to marinate for 10 minutes.

When ready to serve, preheat a griddle pan. Cut the ciabatta into 2cm (¾ inch) slices on the diagonal. Brush with the remaining oil and toast on the griddle pan for 1 minute on each side until lightly charred.

Arrange the hot toasted ciabatta slices on a large platter. Give the tuna and bean salad a big stir and then spoon on top of the toasted ciabatta to serve.

400g can cannellini beans, drained and rinsed
3 spring onions, finely sliced
200g can tuna chunks in olive oil, drained
6 tbsp olive oil
1 lemon, halved with pips removed
2 tbsp chopped fresh flat-leaf parsley
1 large ciabatta loaf
salt and freshly ground black pepper

· ·

Serves 4

GREEK LAMB SALAD WITH RED PEPPER HUMMUS

This salad is a wonderful combination of flavours and textures that is actually incredibly simple to prepare. I like to serve it warm, but of course it would also be good at room temperature, especially as part of a moveable feast. For convenience, buy a jar of roasted red peppers rather than making your own.

4 lamb leg steaks, cut into strips

4 garlic cloves, crushed

1 tsp ground coriander

2 tbsp olive oil

225g (8oz) frozen peas, thawed out

300g (10 ½ oz) feta cheese, crumbled

good handful fresh mint and coriander
   leaves, roughly chopped

couple of handfuls Greek black
   olives, pitted

1 cucumber, diced into about 1cm
   (½ inch) chunks

squeeze of lemon juice

good glug extra virgin olive oil

sea salt and freshly ground
   black pepper

toasted pitta bread, to serve

FOR THE RED PEPPER HUMMUS

400g can chickpeas, drained
   and rinsed

1 roasted red pepper, skinned and
   seeds removed (from a jar is fine)

2 tbsp fresh lemon juice

2 garlic cloves, crushed

1 tsp ground cumin

1 tsp paprika

125ml (4fl oz) tahini paste (sesame
   seed pulp)

2 tbsp extra virgin olive oil

Place the lamb in a shallow dish with the garlic and ground coriander and season to taste. Toss until well coated.

Heat the olive oil in a frying pan. Add the lamb and fry over a high heat for a few minutes until cooked through.

Add the peas to the pan and toss until they are heated through. Tip the contents into a bowl and mix together with the feta, mint, fresh coriander, olives and cucumber. Squeeze over the lemon juice and add a good glug of extra virgin olive oil.

To make the red pepper hummus, place the chickpeas in a food processor or liquidizer with the red pepper, lemon juice, garlic, cumin, paprika, tahini paste and olive oil. Season to taste and blitz to form a thick paste. If the mixture doesn't blend well add a touch of water rather than more oil. Taste and add extra lemon juice, olive oil or spices if you think it needs it.

Arrange the lamb salad on plates with the red pepper hummus and toasted pitta bread to serve.

. . . .

Serves 4

CHICKPEA AND LAMB FALAFEL

ANTONY WORRALL THOMPSON

These falafel are perfect for alfresco eating on a warm summer's day. There's something about being out in the fresh air that stimulates the appetite.

400g can chickpeas, drained
   and rinsed
4 tbsp Greek strained yoghurt
1 tbsp chopped fresh flat-leaf parsley
juice of 1 lemon
2 garlic cloves, finely chopped
1 large onion, roughly chopped
5 tbsp olive oil
200g (7oz) minced lamb
1 tsp ground cumin
1 tsp ground coriander
1 tsp cayenne pepper
1 tbsp chopped fresh coriander
salt and freshly ground black pepper

FOR THE FLATBREAD
200g (7oz) plain flour, plus extra
   for dusting
1 tsp salt

FOR THE WATERCRESS SALAD
1 bunch watercress
squeeze lemon juice
1 tbsp olive oil

. . . .

Serves 4

To make the hummus, place half of the chickpeas in a food processor with the yoghurt, parsley, half of the lemon juice and garlic, one third of the onion and two tablespoons of the olive oil. Blend until smooth and season to taste. Transfer to a bowl, cover with cling film and set aside until needed.

To make the flatbread, put the flour and salt in a large bowl and mix to combine. Add 50ml (2fl oz) of water, a little at a time, mixing all the time with your hand until you have a firm dough and there is no flour left in the bowl. Transfer the dough to a floured surface and knead until it becomes elastic. Put back in the bowl and cover with a damp tea towel. Leave for 10–15 minutes to rest.

To make the lamb falafel, heat one tablespoon of the olive oil in a large frying pan. Place the lamb in a food processor or liquidizer with the other half of the chickpeas, lemon juice and garlic. Add the cumin, ground coriander, cayenne pepper, the rest of the onion, the fresh coriander and the two remaining tablespoons of olive oil.

Blitz the falafel ingredients to a smooth paste. Shape the mix into small patties and flatten out slightly. Fry the falafels for 2–3 minutes on each side or until cooked through.

Meanwhile, heat a large frying pan or flat griddle. Transfer the dough back to a floured surface and knead again. Roll out into a long sausage shape and cut off 2cm (¾ inch) discs. Roll each disc into a ball, then flatten and roll out with a rolling pin until you have a thin disc. Place in the pan and cook for a minute or so on each side until golden and starting to bubble. Repeat until all of the flat bread has been cooked.

Place the watercress in a large bowl and quickly dress with the lemon juice and olive oil. Season to taste and mix well.

Serve the falafel on a bed of watercress salad with the hummus and flatbread on the side.

THAI-STYLE CHICKEN, PRAWN AND CORN CAKES

It's amazing how years ago we all had a local curry restaurant on the corner of our street. Now it seems to be a Thai one! This is a version of one of the most popular dishes, Thai fishcakes. I've combined chicken and prawns to make a delicious starter or light lunch. You can vary the amount of curry paste you use depending on how hot you like your food.

Roughly chop the chicken breast fillets and place in the bowl of a food processor or liquidizer. Add the prawns, egg white, garlic and curry paste. Process until finely chopped.

Tip the chicken paste into a bowl, then add the breadcrumbs, sweetcorn, spring onions and coriander and mix until well combined. Use wet hands to shape the mixture into approximately 16 patties.

To make the sweet chilli sauce, mix the sweet chilli sauce, soy sauce and Thai Fish sauce together in a small bowl. Add the cucumber, if using, and set aside.

Heat the oil in a large frying pan. Add the patties a few at a time and cook for 1–2 minutes on each side until golden brown and cooked through.

Arrange the Thai-style chicken, prawn and corn cakes on plates and put the sweet chilli sauce in dipping bowls on the side to serve.

2 skinless chicken breast fillets

250g (9oz) raw tiger prawns, peeled and de-veined

1 egg white

1 garlic clove, crushed

1–3 tbsp Thai red curry paste

50g (2oz) fresh white breadcrumbs

200g (7oz) can sweetcorn, drained

4 spring onions, sliced

2 tbsp chopped fresh coriander

2 tbsp sunflower oil

1 lime, cut into wedges

FOR THE SWEET CHILLI SAUCE

4 tbsp sweet chilli sauce

1 tsp soy sauce

1 tsp Thai fish sauce (nam pla)

5cm (2 inch) piece cucumber, peeled, seeded and finely chopped (optional)

. . . .

Serves 4

puds

ANTONY WORRALL THOMPSON

HOT CHOCOLATE SOUFFLES WITH RASPBERRY SAUCE

The uncooked soufflé mix can be prepared up to 45 minutes in advance and kept at room temperature before baking. The soufflés won't rise quite as well, but are just as delicious – call them chocolate puddings and nobody will be any the wiser!

Preheat the oven to 220C/425F/Gas 7 and heat a large baking sheet. Butter six individual ramekins or ovenproof teacups then sprinkle with caster sugar inside, shaking off any excess. Chill until required.

Melt the chocolate in a heatproof bowl over a pan of simmering water. Beat in the four egg yolks, one at a time, until the mix thickens.

Whisk the eight egg whites in a separate bowl until stiff, then whisk in the caster sugar, one tablespoon at a time. Fold a little of the egg white mix into the chocolate mix, then fold the chocolate mix into the remaining whisked egg whites until evenly combined.

Divide the mix between the prepared ramekins, then run your finger between the inside edge of each ramekin and the mixture to make a small groove – this helps the soufflé to rise evenly. Place the ramekins on the preheated baking sheet on the top shelf of the oven. Bake for 12–13 minutes until well risen and just wobbly when lightly moved.

Meanwhile, make the raspberry sauce. Purée the raspberries in a food processor or liquidizer, then pass through a sieve into a pan. Add the icing sugar, wine and lemon juice, stirring well to combine. Bring to a simmer and cook for 4–5 minutes until slightly reduced.

Dust the soufflés with icing sugar and serve with the warm raspberry sauce.

25g (1oz) butter, at room temperature

115g (4oz) golden caster sugar, plus a little extra for dusting

300g (10½ oz) plain chocolate (at least 70% cocoa solids) broken into pieces

4 eggs, separated

4 egg whites

icing sugar, for dusting

FOR THE RASPBERRY SAUCE

200g (7oz) raspberries

85g (3oz) icing sugar

85ml (3fl oz) red wine

1 tbsp fresh lemon juice

. . . .

Serves 6

SUMMER FRUIT AND LEMONGRASS BROCHETTE

This is an incredibly easy pudding, best made in the summer when British strawberries are cheap and at their best. It also has the benefit of having no added sugar, making it a good dessert for dieters, served without the ice cream of course!

4 lemongrass stalks, trimmed
8 strawberries, stalks removed
1 large banana
2 ripe peaches
4 tsp finely ground black pepper
4 fresh mint sprigs, plus extra
    to decorate
vanilla ice cream, to serve

. . . .

Serves 4

Preheat the oven to 220C/425F/Gas 7. Peel the banana and cut into eight equal sized pieces. Cut the peaches in half, removing the stone, and cut each half again. Skewer a strawberry, banana piece and peach segment onto each lemongrass stalk and then repeat the process.

Place each skewer in the centre of a circle of tin foil. Sprinkle the black pepper all over the brochettes, turning over to ensure they're well covered. Add a mint sprig to each parcel. Crimp the edges of foil together to form a Cornish pasty shape, ensuring it's sealed all the way around. Place the parcels on a large baking sheet and cook in the oven for 7–8 minutes until the brochettes are heated through and fragrant.

Remove the cooked parcels from the oven, carefully open the foil and roll back the edges to form an oval bowl. Place a scoop or two of ice cream on top of the hot brochettes, decorate with mint and serve.

JEAN-CHRISTOPHE NOVELLI

STRAWBERRY COMPOTE WITH WHITE CHOCOLATE ICE CREAM

JEAN-CHRISTOPHE NOVELLI

This is a basic recipe for a compôte, and you could use any soft fruit that is available and in season, such as raspberries, blackberries, apricots or cherries. However, for me the love affair between the flavours of strawberries and white chocolate has always been intense; they belong together.

To make the strawberry compôte, heat a heavy-based frying pan. Add the vanilla pod and heat for 20 seconds, then add the strawberries and heat for a further 30 seconds. Sprinkle over the sugar and gently stir until it has dissolved. Add the kirsch and allow to warm through. Transfer to a bowl and leave to cool, then cover with cling film and chill until needed.

To make the white chocolate ice cream, gently melt the white chocolate in a heatproof bowl set over a pan of simmering water, using a spatula to stir it – do not allow the chocolate to get too hot.

Once the chocolate has melted, place the bowl on a damp cloth to prevent it from slipping. Slowly pour in the cream, stirring continuously, to form a thick, creamy mixture. Transfer to a rigid plastic container with a lid and freeze for at least 2 hours or overnight is fine.

Remove the white chocolate ice cream from the freezer 30 minutes before you want to serve it and place in the fridge to soften (or 10 minutes at room temperature). Remove the strawberry compôte from the fridge as well and allow it to come back up to room temperature.

Spoon some strawberry compôte into the base of pretty glasses. Discard the vanilla pod. Top with some of the white chocolate ice cream. Repeat with another layer of strawberries and finish with the white chocolate ice cream. Top each one with two tablespoons of crème fraîche and gently tap the glass on the work surface until the top is smooth. Dust with the cocoa powder and serve.

1 vanilla pod, split in half lengthways

500g (1lb 2oz) strawberries, stalks removed and halved

1 tbsp light muscovado sugar

3 tbsp kirsch

8 tbsp low fat crème fraîche

cocoa powder, for dusting

FOR THE WHITE CHOCOLATE ICE CREAM

400g (14oz) good quality white chocolate, broken into small pieces

400ml (14fl oz) double cream, well chilled

....

Serves 4

CREME BRULEE WITH MIXED BERRY COMPOTE

The great thing about this version of a crème brûlée is the lovely puddle of fruity caramel juices at the bottom of the pot that soak into the custard. Use the best quality vanilla pods – Bourbon if you can get them.

8 egg yolks
55g (2oz) caster sugar
568ml (1 pint) double cream
1 vanilla pod, split in half lengthways
4 tbsp Demerara sugar

FOR THE MIXED BERRY COMPOTE
1 vanilla pod, split in half lengthways
115g (4oz) strawberries, stalks removed and halved if large
115g (4oz) blackberries
115g (4oz) raspberries
1 tbsp caster sugar
2 tbsp kirsch

. . . .

Serves 6

To make the compôte, heat a heavy-based frying pan. Add the vanilla pod, and heat for about 20 seconds to release the aroma. Add the berries and heat for another minute or so. Sprinkle over the sugar and toss together until melted. Heat for 1 minute, then add the kirsch and heat through for 30 seconds. Remove from the heat. Divide the compôte between six ramekins and leave to cool.

Preheat the oven to 180C/350F/Gas 4. To make the crème brûlée mix together the egg yolks and sugar in a large bowl. Pour the cream into a pan and scrape in the vanilla seeds, then add the pod. Bring the cream and vanilla mixture to the boil.

Whisk the hot cream into the egg yolks and sugar mixture, then pour back into a clean pan. Heat gently for 2–3 minutes until the custard begins to thicken to the consistency of single cream. Remove and discard the vanilla pod.

Pour the crème brûlée mixture into the ramekins containing the compôte. Stand these on newspaper in a roasting tin and surround with warm water which comes three-quarters of the way up the sides of the ramekins. Cook in the oven for 20–30 minutes until just beginning to set, but there should still be a slight movement in the centre of the custard. Remove from the oven and allow to cool. Place in the fridge and leave to set for a minimum of 6 hours and preferably overnight.

Preheat the grill to its highest setting (or you can use a blowtorch). Sprinkle the crème brûlées with the Demerara sugar, making sure you take it right to the edges of the ramekins, and slide them under the grill for 2–3 minutes until the sugar has caramelized. Remove and leave until the sugar crust has cooled and hardened before serving.

BAKED PEACHES WITH AMARETTI

ANTONY WORRALL THOMPSON

Look out for ripe peaches for this pudding. To test for ripeness, sniff rather than squeeze: the aroma should be fragrant and sweet. It should be possible to find decent fruit from May until October although there is no doubt that the best for flavour are the Italian and French ones, which are available at the height of the summer.

85g (3oz) unsalted butter
4 large ripe peaches
12 amaretti biscuits
2 tbsp toasted flaked almonds
2 tbsp light muscovado sugar
1 tsp ground ginger
85ml (3fl oz) Amaretto (almond liqueur)
125ml (4fl oz) freshly squeezed
   orange juice
vanilla ice cream, to serve

. . . .

Serves 4

Preheat the oven to 190C/375F/Gas 5. Lightly butter a baking dish with 15g (½oz) of the butter.

Place the peaches in a large bowl and cover with boiling water. Leave them for 30–60 seconds and then drain and cover with ice cold water. Peel off the skins, cut in half to remove the stones and then arrange cut-side up in the buttered baking dish.

Place the amaretti biscuits in a food processor or liquidizer with the almonds, sugar and ground ginger, then pulse until crumbled. Add the remaining butter and the Amaretto and pulse again to a paste.

Place a teaspoon of the amaretti mixture into the centre of each peach half and then pour the orange juice around them. Bake for 20–25 minutes, basting with a little orange juice from time to time.

Arrange the peaches with a little of the juices in warmed bowls and add scoops of vanilla ice cream to serve.

TARTE TATIN

JEAN-CHRISTOPHE NOVELLI

This is not as difficult to make as you'd think, and works just fine with bought puff pastry. It's best to allow the tarte tatin to cool a little before serving. This enables all the juices to be reabsorbed and allows the caramel to set slightly because of the pectin in the apples.

Line a tarte tatin mould or deep ovenproof pan with non-stick parchment paper. Roll out the pastry on a lightly floured surface to a round, 2.5cm (1 inch) larger than the top of the mould. Place the pastry on a baking sheet lined with non-stick parchment paper and chill for at least 30 minutes.

Preheat the oven to 220C/425F/Gas 7. Place the butter and sugar in a small heavy-based pan and heat gently, stirring until the sugar has dissolved. To prevent it from caramelizing, add the white wine vinegar. Add the star anise and vanilla seeds and bring to the boil, then simmer for 5 minutes without stirring until you have a rich golden brown caramel. Pour the caramel into the lined mould or pan.

Peel, halve and core the apples and then slice 1 cm (½ inch) layer from the top of the apples so that they are level with the top of the mould. Place, flat side down, in the caramel and bake for 15 minutes until just tender, basting occasionally. Lay the chilled pastry sheet on top of the apples, tucking in the edges and turning them down so that when the tart is turned out, the edges will create a rim that will hold the caramel and apple juices. Bake for 18–20 minutes until the pastry is crisp and golden all over.

Leave the tart in the mould for a minute or two, then loosen the edges with a round-bladed knife and invert carefully onto a flat plate. Leave to cool a little if time allows, then cut into slices and serve with scoops of caramel ice cream.

300g (10 ½ oz) ready-made puff pastry, thawed if frozen
a little plain flour, for dusting
150g (5½ oz) unsalted butter
100g (3½ oz) caster sugar
1 tbsp white wine vinegar
3 star anise
2 vanilla pods, split in half lengthways and seeds scraped out
6 Granny Smith apples
caramel ice cream, to serve

Serves 4–6

STEAMED RHUBARB SPONGE PUDDINGS WITH VANILLA CUSTARD

Steamed puddings have to be the ultimate comforting dessert and I'm sure on most people's list of favourite nursery foods. This mixture also makes one 1.2 litre (2 pints) pudding but that would need to be steamed on the hob for 1¾ to 2 hours.

25g (1oz) butter, plus extra for greasing

150g (5½ oz) caster sugar, plus extra for dusting

350g (12oz) rhubarb, trimmed and sliced

3 large eggs, separated

½ vanilla pod, split in half and seeds scraped out

150ml (¼ pint) buttermilk

190g (6½ oz) self-raising flour

½ tsp baking powder

FOR THE VANILLA CUSTARD

125ml (4fl oz) milk

250ml (9fl oz) double cream

1 vanilla pod

4 egg yolks

70g (2½ oz) caster sugar

· ·

Serves 4–6

Preheat the oven to 180C/350F/Gas 4. Butter six 200ml (7fl oz) individual pudding moulds and dust the insides with caster sugar. Slowly dissolve 55g (2oz) of the sugar in 300ml (½ pint) of water in a heavy-based pan over a gentle heat. Boil for 1 minute then add the rhubarb and simmer gently for a few minutes until almost cooked, turning occasionally.

Remove from the heat, cover and leave for several minutes. When cool, transfer 100g (3½oz) of the rhubarb with a little of the syrup to a food processor or liquidizer and blend to a purée. Set aside.

Divide the remaining cooled rhubarb between the moulds. Melt the butter in a small pan or in the microwave and leave to cool a little. Whisk the egg whites in a bowl until stiff. In a separate bowl, whisk the egg yolks and the remaining sugar until light and fluffy. Add the vanilla seeds, then stir in the melted butter and buttermilk. Sift the flour and baking powder into the bowl. Gently mix into the egg yolk mixture to make a smooth batter. Fold in the egg whites. Divide among the prepared moulds, leaving a slight gap at the top of the mould. Arrange in a large roasting tin half filled with hot water and cover in foil. Cook for 30 minutes, rotating the puddings after 15 minutes to ensure they cook evenly.

To make the custard, place the milk in a pan with the cream and vanilla and bring to the boil. Whisk the egg yolks and sugar in a large heatproof bowl until pale and creamy, then whisk in the hot milk. Set the bowl over a pan of simmering water and cook, stirring continuously, until the custard coats the back of a wooden spoon. If the custard becomes lumpy, sieve into a large jug. Cover with cling film to prevent a skin forming.

Remove the rhubarb puddings from the roasting tin and allow to sit for a few minutes. Turn out each sponge into the centre of a wide-rimmed bowl and pour a little of the rhubarb purée over the top. Drizzle with the warm custard to serve.

WHITE CHOCOLATE AND KIRSCH MOUSSE

I make this dessert in the restaurant and it requires a little bit of skill to caramelize the fruit, but you will be rewarded with a very sexy pudding. Try to make it when British soft fruits are in season, from June to September.

250g (9oz) good quality white chocolate, broken into pieces
125ml (4fl oz) kirsch
250ml (9fl oz) double cream, ice cold
85g (3oz) mascarpone cheese
2 tsp Amaretto (almond liqueur)
250g (9oz) strawberries, stalks removed and sliced, plus extra to decorate
150g (5 1/2 oz) raspberries
1 vanilla pod, split in half
40g (1 1/2 oz) caster sugar
cocoa powder, for dusting
icing sugar, for dusting

. . . .

Serves 4

Melt the white chocolate in a heatproof bowl set over a pan of simmering water. Stir in two-thirds of the kirsch, then whisk in the cream. Remove from the heat and leave to cool, stirring occasionally to prevent a skin forming.

Place the mascarpone in a bowl and add the Amaretto, then mix very gently until soft. Set aside.

Heat a large frying pan. Add the strawberries, raspberries and vanilla pod. Flambé with the rest of the kirsch and then sprinkle over the sugar. Allow to caramelize, shaking the pan occasionally to ensure that the fruit is evenly coated. Transfer to a bowl and leave to cool.

Divide the mascarpone mixture into the bottom of dessert glasses and spoon the fruit mixture on top, discarding the vanilla pod. Cover with the white chocolate mousse. Leave to set in the fridge for at least 1 hour.

Dust the mousses with cocoa powder and icing sugar. Decorate with strawberries to serve.

PANFORTE

Panforte is a traditional Italian dessert containing fruits and nuts that dates back to thirteenth-century Siena, in Italy's Tuscany region. I like a small wedge to be served with coffee or a dessert wine after a meal, though some enjoy it with their coffee at breakfast.

Melt 250g (9oz) of the chocolate in a heatproof bowl set over a pan of simmering water. Leave to cool a little.

Beat the egg whites in a large bowl with a whisk for 2 minutes. Fold in the orange peel, almonds, walnuts and 300g (10½oz) of the icing sugar, until evenly distributed. Very gently stir in the melted chocolate.

Line a round dish that is approximately 20cm (8 inch) in diameter and 3–4cm (1¼–1½ inch) deep with clingfilm. Spoon in the chocolate mixture and level out the top with a spatula. Chill for 2 hours until solid.

Melt the remaining chocolate in a heatproof bowl set over a pan of simmering water.

Place the remaining icing sugar in a heavy-based pan with two tablespoons of water. Heat and stir until the sugar has dissolved, then mix in the melted chocolate to form a syrup-like texture.

Invert the panforte onto a flat plate and carefully peel away the cling film. Using a spatula, spread over the chocolate syrup mixture. Leave to set, then give a light dusting of icing sugar. Cut into thin slices to serve.

350g (12oz) plain chocolate, broken into squares
3 egg whites
25g (1oz) dried orange peel
200g (7oz) ground almonds
100g (3½oz) walnuts, crushed
370g (12½oz) icing sugar, plus extra for dusting

. . . .

Serves 4

HAZELNUT PAVLOVA WITH MANGO AND PASSION FRUIT

After cooking, leave the Pavlova in the turned-off oven with the door shut; this will encourage the middle to develop the characteristic Pavlova marshmallowiness. Walnuts can be used instead of hazelnuts in the meringue. Just choose fruit to compliment the walnuts, such as strawberries and ripe peaches in season.

Preheat the oven to 170C/325F/Gas 3. Lay a sheet of non-stick parchment paper on a large flat baking sheet and mark with a 23cm (9 inch) circle.

Whisk the egg whites in a large bowl with an electric whisk on full speed until they are stiff and look like a cloud. Add the sugar, one teaspoonful at a time, still whisking at full speed until it has all been added.

Blend the cornflour and white wine vinegar together in a bowl and fold into the meringue mixture with the hazelnuts. Spoon the mixture into the circle marked on the non-stick parchment paper on the baking sheet and spread out gently so that the meringue forms a 23cm (9 inch) circle, building the sides up well so that they are higher than the middle.

Place the meringue mixture in the oven but immediately reduce the temperature to 150C/300F/Gas 2. Bake the Pavlova for about 1–1¼ hours until firm to the touch and a pale beige colour. Turn off the oven, leaving the Pavlova inside to cool.

Carefully remove the Pavlova from the baking sheet, peeling off the parchment paper and slide onto a flat serving plate.

To make the filling, mix the whipped cream and yoghurt together in a bowl. Cut the passion fruit in half and scoop out the seeds and juice into a separate bowl. Stir in the mango slices. Mix half the fruit with the cream and yoghurt mixture. Spoon into the centre of the Pavlova and decorate with the remaining mango and passion fruit mixture. Leave in the fridge for about 1 hour before serving.

To make the coulis, mix the lemon curd with the scooped out seeds and juice from the passion fruit and serve with the Pavlova.

4 egg whites
225g (8oz) caster sugar
2 tsp cornflour
2 tsp white wine vinegar
55g (2oz) toasted skinned hazelnuts, roughly chopped

FOR THE COULIS
4 tbsp lemon curd
2 passion fruit

FOR THE FILLING
150ml (¼ pint) whipping cream, whipped
200g (7oz) Greek strained yoghurt
4 passion fruit
1 large ripe mango, peeled and cut into slices

. . . .

Serves 6–8

QUEEN OF PUDDINGS

A family classic, this traditional British dessert, consisting of a baked, breadcrumb-thickened egg custard is normally spread with raspberry jam and topped with meringue. However I've used marmalade instead as I'm just so fond of it.

850ml (1½ pints) milk
55g (2oz) butter, plus extra for greasing
200g (7oz) fresh white breadcrumbs
finely grated rind of 1 orange
pinch ground cinnamon
55g (2oz) caster sugar
3 eggs
3 egg yolks
55g (2oz) marmalade

FOR THE MERINGUE
3 egg whites
115g (4oz) caster sugar, plus extra
   for dusting

· ·

Serves 6–8

Preheat the oven to 180C/350F/Gas 4. Heat the milk in a pan with the butter and pour over the breadcrumbs in a large bowl. Leave to soak for a few minutes.

Fold the orange rind into the breadcrumb mixture with the cinnamon, sugar, 3 whole eggs and 3 egg yolks. Pour into a 1.7 litre (3 pint) buttered pie dish. Place in a roasting tin half filled with hot water and bake for 30–40 minutes until set.

Melt the marmalade in a small pan and spread over the set breadcrumb mixture.

To make the meringue, whisk the egg whites in a large bowl until stiff and then fold in the sugar. Pipe or pile on top of the marmalade layer and dust with a little more caster sugar. Bake for another 15–20 minutes until the meringue is set and pale brown in colour.

Serve the queen of puddings warm.

ANTONY WORRALL THOMPSON

TIRAMISU

Mascarpone is a rich creamy cheese that originiated in Lodi in the Lombardy region of Italy. It has a sweetened taste and is famously used in Tiramisú, which is basically a cream cheese and rum 'trifle' with hints of coffee and chocolate. To bring this dessert a touch more up to date I like to serve it in individual glass coffee cups set on saucers but you could always just layer it up in a single glass dish or bowl if you prefer.

Place the egg yolks in a bowl with the caster sugar and beat together until pale and fluffy, using an electric whisk. Add the mascarpone and whisk slowly until the mixture is smooth. Pour in one tablespoon of the Kahlua or coffee liqueur and whisk gently to combine.

Mix the coffee with the rest of the Kahlua in a shallow dish. Dip half of the boudoir or sponge finger biscuits into the coffee mixture and arrange in the bottom of glass coffee cups, breaking the biscuits up as necessary to fit. Spoon over half the mascarpone mixture and sprinkle half the chocolate on top. Repeat the layers and then cover each cup with cling film. Chill for at least 2 hours or up to 24 hours is fine.

Set the tiramisú on saucers and scatter over the chocolate covered coffee beans just before serving.

3 egg yolks

85g (3oz) caster sugar

2 x 250g tubs mascarpone cheese

85ml (3fl oz) Kahlua or other coffee liqueur

200ml (7fl oz) cold strong coffee or espresso

14 boudoir or sponge finger biscuits

25g (1oz) plain chocolate, finely grated

150g (5½ oz) chocolate covered coffee beans

. . . .

Serves 4

LIMONCELLO TART

This tart originates from the south of Italy and it certainly caters for the sweet tooth. If you get this spot-on it's the perfect pudding. You should aim for a soft, tangy lemon filling spiked with juicy plums and a thin, crisp pastry bottom.

To make the shortcrust pastry, sift the flour into a large bowl. Make a well in the centre and put in the butter, egg yolks, sugar and salt. Using your fingertips, bring the mixture together to form a smooth pastry. Gently gather into a ball, wrap in cling film and chill for 20 minutes.

On a floured surface, roll out the pastry to fit a loose-bottomed flan tin that is about 25cm (9 inch) in diameter. Use the pastry to line a buttered flan tin and let it rest in the fridge for at least 2 hours.

Preheat the oven to 180C/350F/Gas 4. Line the pastry with non-stick parchment paper and fill with baking beans, then bake blind for 15 minutes until just cooked through but not coloured. Remove from the oven. Allow to cool before removing the paper and beans.

To prepare the filling, melt the butter in a small pan or in the microwave. Leave to cool. Place the lemon rind and juice in a bowl and add the melted butter with the cream, almonds, sugar and eggs. Using a hand blender, mix together to a smooth paste, then stir in the Limoncello.

Pour the Limoncello mixture into the base and then arrange the plums on top. Bake on the middle shelf for 20 minutes until just set, then switch off the oven and leave to cool in the oven.

To serve, dust with a thick layer of icing sugar and cut into slices.

120g (4oz) butter

finely grated rind and juice of 1 large lemon (unwaxed if possible)

4 tbsp double cream

100g (3 1/2 oz) ground almonds

200g (7oz) sugar

5 eggs

200ml (7fl oz) Limoncello liqueur

6 plums, cut into wedges

FOR THE PASTRY

190g (6 1/2 oz) plain flour, plus extra for dusting

100g (3 1/2 oz) unsalted butter, softened, plus extra for greasing

3 egg yolks

85g (3oz) icing sugar, plus extra for dusting

pinch of salt

Serves 8

LEMON AND VANILLA CURD TARTS WITH BLUEBERRY COMPOTE

I remember my mum making a version of these when I was a child. The lemon curd and cream make a wonderful filling for the crisp pastry bases. I prefer to eat them on the day that they are made.

375g (13oz) sweet shortcrust pastry, shop-bought or home-made

a little plain flour, for dusting

150g (5½ oz) good quality lemon curd

100ml (3½ fl oz) Greek strained yoghurt

150ml (¼ pint) double cream

1 vanilla pod, split in half lengthways and seeds scraped out

2 tbsp icing sugar

curls of lemon rind and fresh mint sprigs, to decorate

FOR THE COMPOTE

1 tsp cornflour

juice of 1 lemon

250g (9oz) blueberries

3 tbsp icing sugar, plus extra for dusting

. . . .

Serves 4–6

Preheat the oven to 200C/400F/Gas 6. Roll out the pastry on a lightly floured surface and use to line four to six individual tartlet tins, depending on the size you choose. Prick the pastry bases several times with a fork and chill in the fridge for about 30 minutes, or place in the freezer for 10 minutes.

Sit the chilled pastry cases on a large baking sheet and line each one with non-stick parchment paper and some baking beans or rice. Place in the oven for about 10 minutes and then remove the beans and bake for a further 5 minutes or until golden and crisp. Remove from the oven and leave to cool.

To make the blueberry compôte, stir the cornflour into the lemon juice in a small pan. Add the blueberries and icing sugar and place over a low-medium heat. Cook until the blueberries are just beginning to burst and their juices run, giving you a rich purple sauce. Remove from the heat and leave to cool.

To make the filling for the tarts, mix together the lemon curd and Greek yoghurt in a bowl. In a separate bowl, whisk together the cream, vanilla seeds and icing sugar until it just thickens to form soft peaks. Gently fold the lemon curd mixture into the cream.

Turn the pastry cases out onto plates and spoon the filling into each one, scattering with curls of lemon rind. Spoon the cooled blueberry compôte over or around the tarts and finish with a dusting of icing sugar and a sprig of mint.

CHEAT'S LEMON SPONGE WITH TOFFEE SAUCE

ANTONY WORRALL THOMPSON

This is an excellent recipe with tons of great variations. For lemon and chocolate sponge, add a tablespoon of cocoa powder to the sponge mixture. For a fudge sauce, replace the chocolate éclairs with 500g (1lb 2oz) of fudge. For lemon and syrup sponge puddings, add two teaspoons of golden syrup to the base of the moulds before adding the sponge mixture and omit the toffee sauce. This version will also work with your favourite jam.

Lightly oil four to six teacups or individual microwave proof pudding basins and line each one with a circle of non-stick parchment paper.

Sift the flour and baking powder into a large bowl. Add the caster sugar, egg, golden syrup, sunflower oil, milk and lemon rind and, using a hand whisk, mix until smooth. Divide among the prepared teacups.

Place the teacups in the microwave on medium power (for a 1000 watt microwave) for 3½ minutes until the sponges are firm to the touch but still look a little wet in the middle. Leave to cool for 3 minutes.

Meanwhile, melt the chocolate éclairs in a small pan with the cream, stirring until smooth.

Turn the sponge puddings out onto warmed plates and spoon over the toffee sauce to serve.

75ml (2½ fl oz) sunflower oil, plus extra
   for greasing
115g (4oz) self-raising flour
pinch baking powder
85g (3oz) caster sugar
1 egg
1 tbsp golden syrup
125ml (4fl oz) milk
finely grated rind of 1 lemon

FOR THE TOFFEE SAUCE
15 Cadbury's chocolate éclairs
150ml (¼ pint) double cream

....

Serves 4–6

CHOCOLATE PUFF PASTRY WITH STRAWBERRY AND MASCARPONE CREAM

This is such a family favourite in our house – it's perfect for Sunday lunch. Just leave out the Amaretto liqueur if you are serving it to children. The only draw back is that there is quite a bit of washing up, but the recipe itself isn't too complicated.

2 eggs, separated
100g (3½ oz) caster sugar
250g (9oz) mascarpone cheese
200ml (7fl oz) double cream
4 tbsp Amaretto (almond liqueur)
150g (5½ oz) strawberries, stalks removed and halved if large
100g (3½ oz) pistachio nuts, crushed
a little melted butter, for brushing

FOR THE PASTRY
400g (14oz) ready made puff pastry, thawed if frozen
85g (3oz) cocoa powder, plus extra for dusting

. . . .

Serves 4

To make the cream, beat the egg yolks and sugar together in a bowl for 3–4 minutes until pale and thickened. Add the mascarpone cheese and continue to beat until thoroughly mixed together.

Whip the cream in a separate bowl and then gently fold into the egg yolk mixture with a metal spoon. Set to one side.

Whisk the egg whites in another bowl to firm peaks, then fold into the mascarpone cream. Stir in the Amaretto and 70g (2½ oz) of the pistachio nuts. Put in fridge for a couple of hours.

Preheat the oven to 180C/350F/Gas 4. Dust 25g (1oz) of the cocoa on a clean work surface and use a rolling pin to flatten the pastry over the powder. Dust another 25g (1oz) on top and then fold into three.

Roll the pastry out until approximately ½cm (¼ inch) thick. Put into the fridge and leave to rest for 1 hour. Brush a baking sheet with butter and place the pastry on top. Brush two tablespoons of cold water on top and dust over whatever cocoa powder is left. Bake for 30 minutes until crisp and lightly golden. To keep the puff pastry flat, place a baking tray on top whilst cooking. Leave to cool.

Cut the pastry into eight rectangles, about 4cm x 8cm (1½ inches x 3 inches). Spoon the cream over one rectangle and then top with a layer of strawberries. Put another pastry layer on top to make a sandwich. Spoon a little more cream on top and decorate with more strawberries and the reserved pistachio nuts. Dust with cocoa and arrange on plates to serve.

COCONUT RICE PUDDING

This light, unusual pudding tastes so good and bears no resemblance at all to school dinners. It would also be delicious with a simple mixed berry compôte flavoured with a splash of cassis.

Preheat the oven to 200C/400F/Gas 6. Place the coconut milk in a heavy-based pan with the cream, milk, rice and sugar. Bring to the boil and then reduce the heat and simmer very gently for about 1 hour or until the rice is just cooked and the liquid has thickened. Remove from the heat.

Whisk the egg white in a bowl until you have soft peaks. Beat the egg yolk into the cooled rice pudding and then fold in the egg white, using a metal spoon. Transfer to an ovenproof dish and bake for 5 minutes until the top is golden brown and bubbling.

Serve the coconut rice pudding straight to the table and allow everyone to help themselves.

400g (14oz) can coconut milk
50ml (2fl oz) cream
50ml (2fl oz) milk
200g (7oz) short grain pudding rice
55g (2oz) sugar
1 egg, separated

Serves 4

CHEF BIOGRAPHIES

ANTONY WORRALL THOMPSON
Antony is a well-known face on our TV screens. He was a *Ready Steady Cook* regular on the BBC for many years and now presents ITV1's *Saturday Cooks* and *Daily Cooks*. He is passionate about organic farming and his restaurants specialize in organic produce.

ED BAINES
Ed Baines is one of the hottest chefs in Britain. He is a co-presenter on UKTV's *Great Food Live!* and a regular guest on *Daily Cooks* and *Saturday Cooks* on ITV1 and *Ready Steady Cook* on BBC2. He is the author of *Entertain*, and also contributes to *BBC Good Food* and *Olive* magazines.

MARY BERRY
Mary Berry is one of UK's best-known and respected cookery writers, a TV cook and Aga expert. She has been the cookery editor of *Housewife* and *Ideal Home* magazines and has published over 60 cookery books. Mary continues to be a contributor on Radio 4's *Woman's Hour* and still makes regular TV appearances.

MARTIN BLUNOS
Martin's Latvian heritage has had a huge influence on his cooking style. He has held two Michelin stars for over 15 years and was chosen to cook for Her Majesty The Queen in her Jubilee year. Martin appears regularly on *Great Food Live!* and *Food Uncut* on UKTV and *Saturday Kitchen* on BBC1.

FRANK BORDONI
Frank sees no reason why healthy food should be dull and his ethos has always been to use the best ingredients simply. He has worked with many respected chefs and runs his own restaurant, *Limoncello*. He also writes regularly for many publications.

MOMMA CHERRI
Charita Jones grew up in Philadelphia. She first came to prominence during the second series of *Ramsay's Kitchen Nightmares* on Channel 4. Her restaurant, *Momma Cherri's Soul Food Shack*, in Brighton sells home-cooked 'soul food' based on family recipes.

GENNARO CONTALDO
Gennaro Contaldo is widely known as the Italian legend who taught Jamie Oliver all he knows about Italian cooking. His quintessentially Italian spirit and positive nature has made him a TV favourite. Gennaro is the Italian food expert on *Richard and Judy* on Channel 4 and a regular on *BBC Breakfast* on BBC1.

GINO D'ACAMPO
Born in Italy, Gino inherited his grandfather's love of cooking. In 2005, he set off on a culinary adventure in Central America for his own series, *An Italian in Mexico* on UKTV. Gino appears regularly on ITV1's *Saturday Cooks* and *Daily Cooks* and is one of the viewers' favourite chefs.

KEITH FLOYD
Keith Floyd needs no introduction; his television shows and books combine cookery and travel together with his special brand of humour and knowledge that have made him so popular.

AINSLEY HARRIOTT
Ainsley is the charismatic and flamboyant presenter of BBC2's *Ready Steady Cook*. He advises people to use fresh ingredients, have everything ready beforehand and never say 'it's too difficult!'

KEN HOM
Ken's first major TV series, *Ken Hom's Chinese Cookery*, for the BBC was a huge success and he has since hosted numerous other TV shows. He has written over 20 books and is now a consultant for many prestigious hotels and restaurants all over the world.

CHING-HE HUANG
Born in Taiwan, educated in South Africa, UK and Italy, Ching has been exposed to a wide range of cuisines. Her cooking fuses traditional and modern Chinese. She regularly appears on UKTV's *Great Food Live!* and *Taste*. She also has her own series, *Ching's Kitchen* and has published her first book, *China Modern*.

ATUL KOCHHAR
At the age of 31 Atul became the first Indian chef to be awarded a coveted Michelin star. Renowned for the vibrancy of his food and the subtlety of his spice mixes, Atul always remains faithful to the origins of his recipes.

KYLIE KWONG
Fourth generation Chinese-Australian, Kylie cooks with energy and passion. She combines traditional family recipes with modern ideas and techniques, resulting in an exciting new blend of Chinese and contemporary Australian cuisine.

PRUE LEITH
Prue Leith was born in South Africa, and was awarded an OBE for her contribution to the food industry in the UK. She has been a cookery editor and food columnist for many newspapers, including the *Daily Mail*, *Sunday Express*, *Guardian* and *Mirror*.

CLODAGH McKENNA
Clodagh McKenna trained as a chef at Ballymaloe Cookery School. She left the kitchen to set up her own stall at a local market and has developed farmers' markets around Ireland. She

has her own weekly column for the *Irish Examiner, The Mail on Sunday* and *Food and Wine Magazine*. Her TV series, *Fresh from the Farmers' Markets* on RTE 1, accompanies her first book, *The Irish Farmers' Market Cookbook*.

MANJU MALHI

Manju was raised in North West London surrounded by Indian culture, tradition and lifestyle. She spent many years in India exploring its varied cuisine. Her cooking draws on her past to create her own unique Brit-Indi style of food which has culminated in three books; *Brit Spice, India with Passion* and *Easy Indian*.

PAUL MERRETT

Paul Merrett trained under some of London's finest chefs. He has twice been awarded a Michelin star at both *L'Interlude* and *Greenhouse* restaurants. Paul is the presenter of the BBC's *Ever Wondered About Food* as well regularly appearing on *Food Network Daily* for the Carlton Food Network and co presenting *Food Uncut* on UKTV. Paul contributes to various magazines and is currently working on his first book.

JEAN-CHRISTOPHE NOVELLI

Jean-Christophe Novelli is a Michelin and 5AA Rosette award winning French chef. He has won Restaurant of the Year on many occasions and his cookery school, the Novelli Academy, is ranked one of the best in the world. He is a regular guest on ITV1's *Daily Cooks* and *Saturday Cooks*.

BEN O'DONOGHUE

Australian-born Ben has worked in many restaurants including *Monte's, Atlantic Bar and Grill* and *River Café*. He co-presented *The Best* on BBC2 and has appeared in many other TV shows. He is the author of three books and has written a regular food column for *Olive* and also for *delicious* in Australia.

MERRILEES PARKER

Merrilees began her TV career as a researcher. She first appeared on BBC1's *Anything You Can Cook*, co-presented by Brian Turner, and has gone on to present her own series, *Food Uncut* on UKTV along with regular guest appearances on BBC1's *Saturday Kitchen*, UKTV's *Great Food Live!* and ITV1's *Daily Cooks* and *Saturday Cooks*. She now runs 'Pink Food', her own catering company.

RICHARD PHILLIPS

Richard's food can best be described as modern French cuisine, producing unique dishes with complimentary flavours, textures and colours. He is chef/patron of *Thackeray's* in Tunbridge Wells and *Hengist*, near Maidstone in Kent. He has appeared on many TV shows including *Food Uncut* on UKTV, *Ready Steady Cook* on BBC2 and *Saturday Cooks* and *Daily Cooks* on ITV1.

JO PRATT

Jo Pratt's quirky, no-fuss recipes and warm, engaging presence make her among the most popular female chefs on our screens. Recently named as one of Waterstone's Authors for the Future, Jo published her cookbook, *In The Mood For Food*, to rave reviews. She is also the food editor for *Glamour* magazine.

GARY RHODES

Gary Rhodes' legendary dedication to his craft and pursuit of perfection have placed him firmly at the forefront of today's culinary world. A history of stunning restaurants has won him a constellation of Michelin stars and he is consistently revered by his peers as 'The Chef's Chef'.

MIKE ROBINSON

Mike Robinson has starred in many TV shows and is the nation's favourite hunter gatherer. Mike's greatest passion is wild food and game. His book, *Wild Flavours,* was published in 2005 and he also writes for *The Field*.

SILVENA ROWE

Feisty and energetic Bulgarian-born Silvena is the leading expert in Central and Eastern European cuisine. Her distinctive style of cooking combines her heritage with a modern British twist. She has worked as a chef, presenter, food writer and culinary consultant. She is the author of *Feasts*, and appears regularly on UKTV's *Great Food Live*, BBC1's *Saturday Kitchen* and ITV1's *Saturday Cooks*.

JUN TANAKA

Jun's dedication to creating good food has led him to train at some of the world's best restaurants. Jun owns his own restaurant, *Pearl*, and also has his own TV show, *Cooking It*, on Channel 4. He believes that, with passion and dedication, anyone can learn to cook.

BRIAN TURNER

Brian Turner is one of TV's most familiar chefs. He owns several restaurants, including *Brian Turner Mayfair* at the Millenium Hotel, and has been awarded a CBE for his services to tourism and training in the catering industry He appears regularly on *Daily Cooks* and *Saturday Cooks* on ITV1 and *Ready Steady Cook* on BBC2.

ALDO ZILLI

No one has done more to popularise Italian cookery using fish than Aldo Zilli. He now owns five restaurants, ranging from the elegant *Signor Zilli* in Soho to funky *Zilli Fish Too* on Drury Lane. and he won Best Italian Restaurant at the London Restaurant Awards. He is the author of four books, most recently *Fish Cook*, and appears regularly on television.

INDEX